WinQSB Version 2.0

WinQSB Version 2.0

Software by YIH-LONG CHANG
Georgia Institute of Technology

Manual by KIRAN DESAI
University of Memphis

with contributions by
Thomas Kratzer, Malone College

WILEY

JOHN WILEY & SONS, INC

ACQUISITIONS EDITOR	Beth Lang Golub
ASSISTANT EDITOR	Lorraina Raccuia
MARKETING MANAGER	Gitti Lindner
PRODUCTION EDITOR	Lenore Belton
DESIGNER	Karin Kincheloe

To order books or for customer service call 1-800-CALL-WILEY (225-5945).

ISBN 0-471-40672-4

Printed in the United States of America

10 9 8 7 6

Printed and bound by Von Hoffmann Graphics, Inc.

PREFACE

There is an increased using spreadsheets — such as Excel, Lotus and QuatroPro — for solving basic linear programming and other types of problems or converting applications into LP type formulations. When this is done in a class, the instructor ends up spending a considerable amount of time teaching the students how to use and navigate spreadsheets. This takes valuable time away from teaching production operations management, management science, decision sciences, and operations research material in the class. I also find that using spreadsheets forces the instructor and students to convert the form of a problem to fit the spreadsheet requirements. Users will find that using WinQSB allows the problem input to correspond to the problem formulation.

This manual is not a substitute for a textbook in management sciences, decision sciences, or operations research. The sole purpose of this manual is to facilitate the basic use of the powerful WinQSB software. No attempt has been made to teach management science, but I've formulated the manual to illustrate how WinQSB can be used with typical management science problems that contain a problem statement, problem formulation, and so on. This manual does not fully explore all of the WinQSB features, so users are encouraged to look into 'Help' function on the toolbar for learning the full features of the WinQSB software. This manual can be used as a stand alone how-to manual for WinQSB or it can be used with any production and operations management, management science, decision sciences, or operations research textbook — particularly Operations Management by Reid and Sanders and Applied Management Science, 2nd Edition by Lawrence and Pasternack.

I would like to dedicate this manual to my high school teacher and mentor, Mr. Govindbhai J. Patel, whose encouragement and interest helped him to become a better student and person. I also want to acknowledge the editorial help from my daughter Shefaali and the feedback provided by my graduate students from the Quantitative Methods class at Fogelman College of Business, University of Memphis. Finally, I would like to thank Thomas Kratzer of Malone College for his technical review of this manual.

CONTENTS

CHAPTER 1

Introduction to WinQSB

Welcome to WinQSB Update Version for an IBM compatible computer, using Windows 95, 98, Me, 2000 Professional or XP operating system. This software package is designed to solve problems in management science, decision science, operations research, and production and operations management.

In this chapter, you will learn to install and use the WinQSB for making decisions for:

Linear programming (LP)

Linear goal programming (GP) and integer linear goal programming (IGP)

Quadratic programming (QP) and integer quadratic programming (IQP)

Network modeling (NET)

Nonlinear programming (NLP)

Dynamic programming (DP)

PERT/CPM

Queuing/ Waiting Lines analysis (QA)

Queuing/Waiting system simulation (QSS)

Inventory theory and systems (ITS)

Forecasting (FC)

Decision analysis (DA)

Markov process (MKP)

      Quality control charts (QCC)

      Acceptance sampling analysis (ASA)

      Job scheduling (JOB)

      Aggregate planning (AP)

      Facility location and layout (FLL)

      Material requirements planning (MRP)

This chapter is organized to guide you through the installation of the software and familiarize you with the some Windows and WinQSB commands. Those who would like to start using the software right away will find these the three basic steps very useful.

- Install the software as described in Getting Started with WinQSB
- Follow the rest of the chapter or glance at the material presented here.
- Select the appropriate application from 19 application programs. Each application is independent from each other; hence, you can go to any application chapter directly.

GETTING STARTED WITH WINQSB

In order to install WinQSB, you will need the following:

- IBM or IBM compatible PC computer
- Windows 95, 98, Me, 2000 professional or XP edition
- At least 10 mb free on hard disk memory
- At least 36 mb RAM memory
- Color monitor
- Laser, color, ink-jet or dot matrix printer if you want to print the results

INSTALLING WINQSB FOR WINDOWS

Here are the steps to install WinQSB for Windows

1. Insert the CD into the CD-ROM drive.
2. In Windows from the Start taskbar, select RUN.

3. On the command line, type D:\Setup (if your CD-ROM drive is designated a different letter enter that letter instead of D).
4. Click the OK button or press Enter key.
5. Follow the prompts on your screen. You may change the directory for the programs. You will have to provide the user name and school or company name, if you have one, during this installation process.
6. After the successful installation, click on the program and select WINQSB, and then select the appropriate application. See figure 1.1.

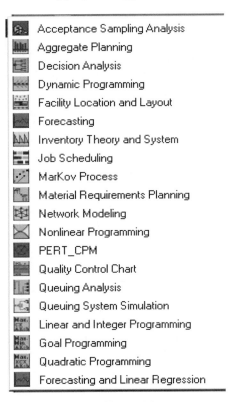

Figure 1.1

Brief Description of the Application Modules

WinQSB includes 19 application modules. Here is an overview of each application. The user who is familiar with these applications will be able to go directly to the application module and will find the use of the software self-explanatory. Data input can be made in spreadsheet format.

1.   **Linear programming (LP) and integer linear programming (ILP):**

This general purpose linear and integer linear programming module will maximize or minimize the value of a linear objective function and limited number of linear constraints. The decision variable may have any continuous value, an integer value or have binary (0 or 1) values. Typical applications include **Linear Programming (LP) and Integer Linear Programming**. One can get a graphic solution (for two decision variables only), final solution or a step-by-step simplex tableau, as well as sensitivity analysis.

2.   **Linear goal programming (GP) and integer linear goal programming (IGP):**

This program solves **Goal programming and Integer Goal Programming** problems where you have more than one linear objective to be satisfied and have a limited number of linear constraints. The goals are either prioritized or ordered. The decision variable may have any continuous value or an integer value or may have binary (0 or 1) values. One can get a graphic solution (for two decision variables only), a final solution or a step-by-step solution, as well as sensitivity analysis.

3.   **Quadratic programming (QP) and integer quadratic programming (IQP).**

This module solves **Quadratic programming and Integer Quadratic Programming** problems, as it has a quadratic objective function and a limited number of linear constraints. Decision variables may be bounded by certain values. One can get a graphic solution (for two decision variables), a final solution or step-by-step solution, as well as a sensitivity analysis.

4.   **Network modeling (NET):**

This module solves network problems such as **capacitated network flow (transshipment), transportation, assignment, maximal flow, minimal spanning tree, shortest path and traveling salesperson** problems. A network model includes nodes and arcs/links (connections).

5. **Nonlinear programming (NLP):**

This module solves a nonlinear objective function with linear and/or nonlinear constraints. The decision variables may be constrained or unconstrained. The NLP can be classified as an unconstrained single variable problem, an unconstrained multiple variables problem and a constrained problem, employing different techniques to solve them.

6. **Dynamic programming (DP):**

Dynamic programming is a mathematical technique for making a sequence of interrelated decisions. Each problem tends to be unique. This module handles three typical dynamic programming problems: knapsack, stagecoach, and production and inventory scheduling.

7. **PERT/CPM:**

This program is for project management. One can use either Program Evaluation and Review Technique (PERT) or Critical Path Method (CAM) or both. A project consists of activities and precedence relations. It will identify critical activities, slacks available for other activities and the completion time of project. It also develops bar (Gantt) charts for activities for visual monitoring.

8. **Queuing analysis:**

This program evaluates a single stage queuing/waiting line system. It allows the user to select from 15 different probability distributions, including Monte Carlo simulation, for inter-arrival service time and arrival batch size. Output constitutes performance measurements of the queuing system, as well as a cost/benefit analysis.

9. **Queuing system simulation (QSS):**

This module performs discrete event simulation of single queuing and multiple queuing systems. The input requirements are customer arrival population, number of servers, queues, and/or garbage collectors (customer leaving the system before completing the service). The output constitutes performance measurements of the queuing system in both tabular form and graphic form.

10. **Inventory theory and systems (ITS):**

This program solves and evaluates inventory control systems, including the conventional EOQ model, quantity discount model, stochastic inventory model, Monte Carlo simulation of inventory control system and the single period model.

11. **Forecasting (FC):**

This module provides eleven different forecasting models. Output includes forecast, tracking signal and error measurements. The data and forecast are also displayed in graphical form.

12. **Decision analysis (DA):**

This module solves four decision problems: Bayesian, decision tree, payoff tables and zero-sum game theory (game play and Monte Carlo simulation).

13. **Markov process (MKP):**

A system exists in different conditions (states). Over time, the system will move from one state to another state. The Markov process will give a probability of going from one state to another state. A typical example could be brand switching by a consumer. Here the module will solve for steady state probabilities and analyze total cost or return.

14. **Quality control charts (QCC):**

This module performs statistical analysis and constructs quality control charts. It will construct 21 different control charts, including X-bar, R chart, p chart, and C chart. It also performs process capability analysis. Output is displayed in both table form and graph form.

15. **Acceptance sampling analysis (ASA):**

This module develops and analyzes acceptance-sampling plans for attribute and variable quality characteristics, such as single sampling, multiple sampling etc. It will construct OC, AOQ, ATI; ASN cost curves and can perform what-if analyses.

16.   **Job scheduling (JOB):**

This module solves scheduling problems for a job shop and a flow shop. There are 15 priority rules available for job shop scheduling, including the best solution based on selected criterion. Seven popular heuristics are available for flow shop scheduling, including the best solution based on selected criterion. Output can be viewed both in tabular form and on a Gantt chart.

17.   **Aggregate planning (AP):**

Aggregate planning deals with capacity planning and production schedule to meet demand requirements for the intermediate planning horizon. Typical decisions are aggregate production, manpower requirements and scheduling, inventory levels, subcontracting, backorder and /or lost sales.

18.   **Facility location and layout (FLL):**

This module evaluates the facility location for a two or three-dimensional pattern (plant and/or warehouse), facility design for functional (job shop) layout and production line (flow shop). The facility location finds the location, which minimizes the weighted distance. Functional facility design is based on modified CRAFT algorithm. For flow shop design (line balancing), three different algorithms are available.

19.   **Material requirement planning (MRP):**

This module addresses the issues related to material requirement planning (MRP) for production planning. Based on final demand requirements, both in terms of how many and when products will be delivered to customers, the MRP method will determine net requirements, planned orders, and projected inventory for materials and components items. This module will perform capacity analysis, cost analysis, and inventory analysis.

USING WINQSB

This section describes the common features of all 19 modules of WinQSB.

Selecting an application

After starting WinQSB, (see figure 1.2), select the application you want to execute.

Figure: 1.2

You will see the screen with a tool bar consisting of file and help (see figure 1.2). In the file pull down menu, you will see the following options:

New problem
Load problem (*previously saved problems*)
Exit

Once the problem is entered, the tools bar will look like figure 1.3 (More discussion of this later on).

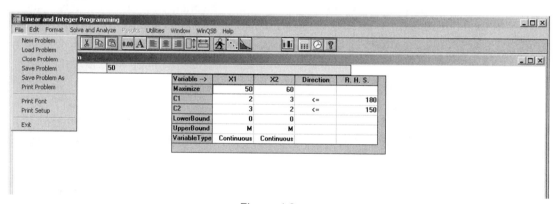

Figure: 1.3

Now the **file menu** includes the following commands:

New Problem: to start a new problem
Load Problem: to open and load a previously saved problem
Close Problem: to close the current problem

Save Problem: to save the current problem with the current file name

Save Problem As: to save the current problem under a new name

Print Problem: to print the problem

Print Font: to select the print font

Print Setup: to setup the print page

Exit: to exit the program

The next item on the tool bar is the **Edit menu**. It has the following commands:

Cut: to copy the selected areas in the spreadsheet to the clipboard and clear the selected area

Copy: to copy the selected areas in the spreadsheet to the clipboard

Paste: to past the content of the clipboard to selected areas in the spreadsheet

Clear: to clear the selected areas in the spreadsheet

Undo: to undo the above action

Problem Name: to change the problem name

Other commands, which appear here, are applicable to the particular application you are using.

Format menu: this pull-down menu includes following commands:

Number: to change the number format for the current spreadsheet or grid

Font: to change the font for the current spreadsheet or grid

Alignment: to change the alignment for selected columns or rows of the current spreadsheet or grid

Row Height: to change the height for the selected rows of the current spreadsheet or grid

Column Width: to change the width for the selected columns of the current spreadsheet or grid

Other commands, which appear here, are applicable to the particular application you are using (more later on).

Solve and analyze menu: this pull-down menu typically includes the following commands:

Solve the Problem: to solve the problem and display the results

Solve and Display Steps: to solve and display the solution iterations step by step

Result menu: this includes the options to display the solution results and analyses.

Utility menu: this pull-down menu includes following commands:

Calculator: pops open the Windows system calculator
Clock: display the Windows system clock
Graph/Chart: to call a general graph and chart designer

Widow menu: this pull-down menu includes following commands:

Cascade: to cascade windows for the current problem
Tile: to tile all windows for the current problem
Arrange Icons: to arrange all windows if they are minimized to icons

WinQSB menu: this pull-down menu includes following commands: this includes the option to switch to another application module without shutting down the WinQSB program (see figure 1.4).

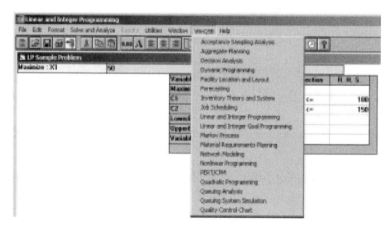

Figure: 1.4

Help menu: this pull-down menu includes following commands:

Contents: to display the main help categories in the help file

Search for Help on: to start the search for a keyword in the help file

How to Use Help: to start the standard Windows help instruction

Help on Current window: to display the help for the current window. You can click any area of the window to display more information

About the Program: to display the short information about the program

In this chapter, we have given an overview of WinQSB. The remaining chapters in this manual cover each application module with complete illustration using basic examples.

CHAPTER 2

Linear Programming (LP) and Integer Linear Programming (ILP)

This programming module solves linear programming (LP) and integer linear programming (ILP) problems. Both LP and ILP problems have one linear objective function and set of linear constraints. Decision variables for LP problems are continuous (that is not an integer) and usually non-negative. Decision variables for ILP problems are either integer or binary (0 or 1), or one can have mixed integer linear programming problems where the some decision variables could be continuous, some could be binary and others could be integer. Decision variables may be bounded with limited values.

The LP module uses simplex and graphical methods for solving problems. If the LP problem consists of two decision variables, one can use either of the methods to solve it. A LP problem with more than two decision variables is solved using the simplex method. The ILP module uses a branch-and-bound method for solving problems.

Let's walk through an example problem. Here we will examine a problem, formulate a LP/ILP model, make an input to the WinQSB LP/ILP module, and analyze the output.

CMP is a cherry furniture manufacturer. Their primary products are chairs and tables. CMP has a limited supply of wood available for making chairs and tables. Each week their suppler provides them with 100 board feet of cherry wood. Each chair requires 4 board feet of wood and a table needs 6 board feet. CMP can sell all the chairs and tables it can make. CMP has at their disposal only 120 man-hours available per week for making the furniture. It takes 4.5 man-hours to make a chair and 5 man-hours to make a table. CMP makes $30 profit for every chair it sells and makes $35 profit for every table sold. Here CMP wants to decide how many chairs and tables it should make to maximize total profits.

Problem formulation
Data summary

Product	Wood needed (board feet)	Man-hours	Profit per piece
Chair	4	4.5	$30
Table	6	5	$35
Available Resources	100	120	

Step 1. Define the decision variables:
   Let C be the number chairs produced.
   Let T be the number of tables produced.

Step 2. Objective function:
   Maximize total profit: $30C + $ 35T

Step 3. Subjective to constraints:
   4C + 6T <= 100   Wood available constraint
   4.5C + 5T <= 120   Man-hours available
   C, T >= 0   Non negativity constraints

LP model:
   Let C be number chairs produced.
   Let T be number of tables produced.
   Maximize total profit: $30C + $ 35T
   Subject to   4C + 6T <= 100   Wood available constraint
                  4.5C + 5T <= 120   Man-hours available
                  C, T >= 0   Non negativity constraints

Once the LP model is developed, you are ready to solve it using WinQSB. At "start," click the left mouse button. At the pop-up menu, click the mouse on "Programs." You will see a menu with WinQSB on it; click the mouse on it and you will see all WinQSB modules. Select Linear and Integer Programming. On the toolbar, click on the file and then on New Problem. The menu will appear as shown in Figure 2.1. Enter the Problem

Title, Number of variables, Number of Constraints, then select under Objective Criterion, Maximization, under Default Variable Type, Nonnegative continuous (we will discuss this in another selection later in this manual).

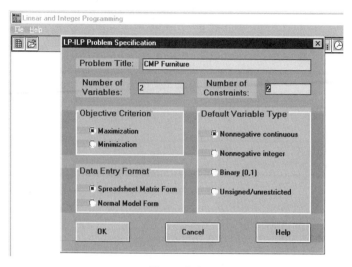

Figure 2.1

Now you have the option of entering data in either the Spreadsheet Matrix Form or the Normal Model Form. My recommendation is that you start with first option (See Figure 2.1).

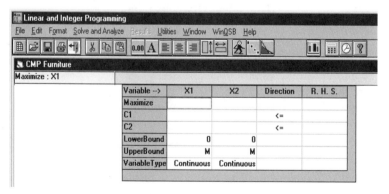

Figure 2.2

Click OK and you will see a screen as shown in Figure 2.2, ready to make data input in the spreadsheet form. In the variable row, you will see the decision variables as X1 and X2, and C1 and C2 represent the two constraints (these are default values). You can change all these by clicking "Edit" on the Toolbar (Figure 2.3). Here you can change decision variables name by selecting Variable Names and the constraint names by selecting Constraint Name (See Figure 2.4). Now you can enter data just like in the CMP LP model. You can enter a number and Tab to the next cell for number entry (just like in Microsoft EXCEL).

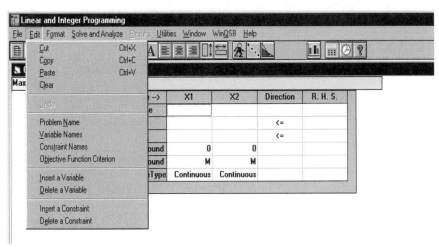

Figure 2.3

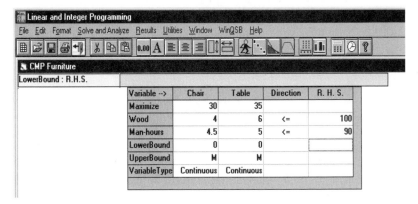

Figure 2.4

Once you have completed the data entry, click on "Solve and Analyze" on the Toolbar (Figure 2.5). Here you will get the option of solving the LP problem, Solve the Problem (this option will give you a final solution using simplex algorithm, including sensitivity analysis), Solve and Display Steps (this option will display step (tableau) by step (tableau) Simplex algorithm output), and Graphic Method (graphical display of solution for two decision variables problem only).

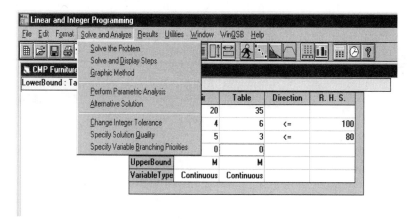

Figure 2.5

First, look at the graphical solution as shown in Figure 2.6. The gray line represents two constraints, Wood and Man-hours. The dark line is the objective function line at the optimal solution. The shaded area identifies the feasible region. Here we have an optimal solution with an object function value (profit maximization) of $621.43, the number chairs to be produced equal to 5.71 and the number tables to be made equal to 12.86.

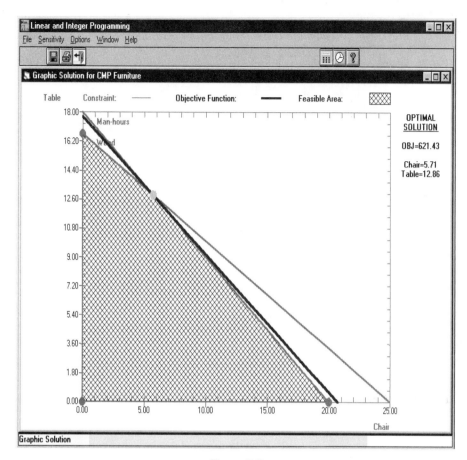

Figure 2.6

The same solution can be obtained by selecting the option "Solve the Problem" on the Solve and Analyze Toolbar. Output of this option is shown in Figure 2.7. Here one gets both the solution as well as the sensitivity analysis of the LP problem.

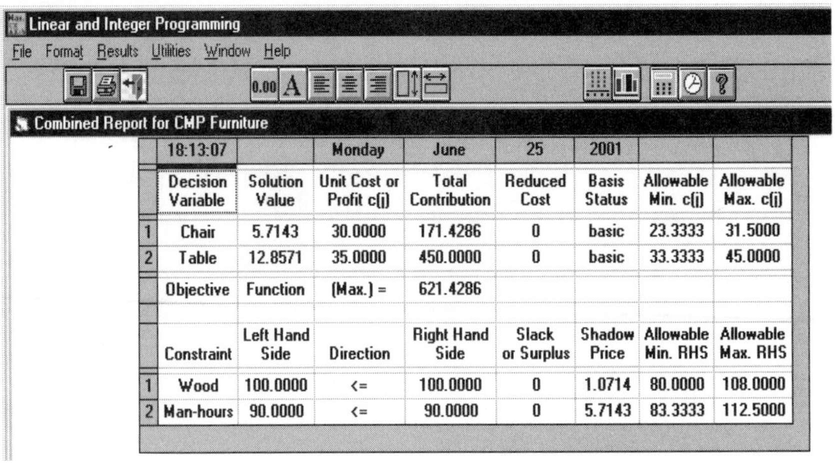

Linear and Integer Programming

File Format Results Utilities Window Help

Combined Report for CMP Furniture

18:13:07		Monday	June	25	2001		
Decision Variable	Solution Value	Unit Cost or Profit c(j)	Total Contribution	Reduced Cost	Basis Status	Allowable Min. c(j)	Allowable Max. c(j)
1 Chair	5.7143	30.0000	171.4286	0	basic	23.3333	31.5000
2 Table	12.8571	35.0000	450.0000	0	basic	33.3333	45.0000
Objective	Function	(Max.) =	621.4286				
Constraint	Left Hand Side	Direction	Right Hand Side	Slack or Surplus	Shadow Price	Allowable Min. RHS	Allowable Max. RHS
1 Wood	100.0000	<=	100.0000	0	1.0714	80.0000	108.0000
2 Man-hours	90.0000	<=	90.0000	0	5.7143	83.3333	112.5000

Figure 2.7

Initially if you want to use the LP Model Form input instead of the Spreadsheet Matrix Form, select the option Normal Model Form, in the LP/ILP Problem Specification menu (Figure 2.8). An experienced user may find this option familiar. Once this option is selected, the screen will display the input format as shown in Figure 2.9. In this option, you will have to use X1 and X2 (default notations) as decision variables for the CMP problem (or any other LP problems) as input and then change the names of the decision variables using the Edit option from the Toolbar as well as for constraints. See Figures 2.10 and 2.11.

Figure 2.8

Figure 2.9

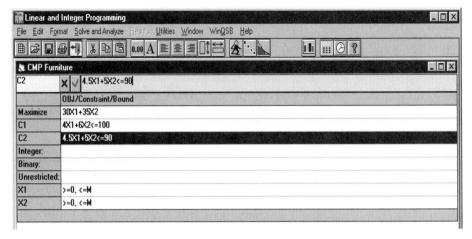

Figure 2.10

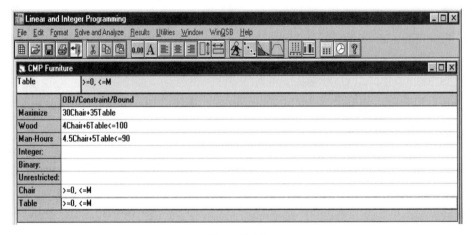

Figure 2.11

In this solution, one would observe that the numbers of chairs and tables to be produced are not integer. This would be OK if one is involved in long term production, just like an automobile maker, but if this is not the case, then one would like to ensure that the numbers of chairs and tables to be produced are an integer value. This brings us to the Integer Linear Programming problem.

We can use the same data and modify the variable type as shown in Figure 2.4. Go to the Variable Type in the Chair column and right click the mouse. You will notice that the variable type value will change from continuous to Integer. Do the same thing under the

Table column. Now Solve and Analyze this problem. (You could have selected variable type as an Integer at the time of starting this problem as the option shown in Figure 2.2). The screen output is shown in Figure 2.12. The Integer LP solution for the CMP Furniture problem consists of producing 10 chairs and 9 tables with a profit equal to $615, as compared to the LP solution of producing 5.71 chairs and 12.85 tables with a profit of $621.42.

Linear and Integer Programming

File Format Results Utilities Window Help

Combined Report for CMP Furniture

22:04:15			Monday	June	25	2001
	Decision Variable	Solution Value	Unit Cost or Profit c(j)	Total Contribution	Reduced Cost	Basis Status
1	Chair	10.0000	30.0000	300.0000	0	basic
2	Table	9.0000	35.0000	315.0000	0	basic
	Objective	Function	(Max.) =	615.0000		
	Constraint	Left Hand Side	Direction	Right Hand Side	Slack or Surplus	Shadow Price
1	Wood	94.0000	<=	100.0000	6.0000	0
2	Man-hours	90.0000	<=	90.0000	0	6.6667

Figure 2.12

Now you can print the problem by clicking on the print icon (or click on file and from the pop down menu click on print) on the tool bar. To print the solution out at the time of the display of the solution, click on the print icon. You also have the option of printing only the solution summary, the constraint summary, the sensitivity analysis for objective function (OBJ), the sensitivity analysis for right hand side (RHS), or the final Simplex Tableau by clicking on "Results" on the tool bar and selecting the appropriate option from the pop down menu.

After obtaining the solution, if you want to edit the problem for "what if" analysis, you can click on "Window" on the tool bar and from the pop down menu select the problem name, and this will display the problem as entered in Figure 2.1. Now you can edit any part of the inputs by simply clicking on it.

If you need further help with this module then click on "Help" on the tool bar and select an appropriate category by clicking on it.

CHAPTER **3**

Linear Goal Programming (GP) and Integer Linear Goal Programming (IGP)

This programming module solves linear goal programming (GP) and integer linear goal programming (IGP) problems. Both GP and IGP have more than one objective or goal to be achieved simultaneously subject to linear constraints. The objective of GP and IGP programming is to find a solution that satisfies the constraints and, if this is not possible, comes close to meeting the goals.

The GP module uses simplex and graphical methods for solving problems. If the GP problem consists of two decision variables, one can use either of the methods to solve it. A GP problem with more than two decision variables is solved using the simplex method. The IGP module uses a branch-and bound method for solving problems.

Let's walk through an example problem. Here we will examine a problem, formulate a GP/IGP model, input data into the WinQSB GP/IP module, and analyze the output.

CMP is a cherry furniture manufacturer. Their primary products are chairs and tables. CMP has limited supply of wood available for making chairs and tables. Each week their supplier provides them with 100 board feet of cherry wood. Each chair requires 4 board feet of wood, and a table needs 6 board feet. CMP can sell all the chairs and tables it can make. CMP has at their disposal only 120 man-hours (regular time plus overtime) available per week for making the furniture. It takes 4.5 man-hours to make a chair and 5 man-hours to make a table. CMP makes a $30 profit for every chair it sells and makes $35 profit for every table sold. Here CMP wants to decide how many chairs and tables it should make to maximize its total profits. The owner also wishes to meet a prioritized need of:

1. To make at least $700 profit
2. Produce at least 10 tables
3. Use no more than 100 hrs of labor

GP model:

Let C be the number of chairs produced.
Let T be the number of tables produced.
Maximize total profit: $30C + $35T
Subject to $4C + 6T <= 100$ Wood available constraint
                  $4.5C + 5T <= 120$ Man-hours available.
                  $C, T >= 0$ Non negativity constraints.

Goals to be achieved:

$30C+$35T+U1-E1= $700 (profit goal)
$T + U2-E2 = 10$ (chair production goal)
$4.5C+5T +U3-E3 = 100$ (labor-hour goal)
(Where U_i = the amount by which the left side falls short of (under)
Its right-hand side value, E_i = the amount by which the left side
Exceeds its right-hand side value)

Priority given to these goals:

Priority 1: Under achieving $700 profit   U1
Priority 2: Under achieving 10 chair production   U2
Priority 3: Using more than 100 man-hours   E3

Thus, the corresponding priority objectives are:

Priority 1: Minimize U1
Priority 2: Minimize U2
Priority 3: Minimize E3

This example consists of three goals: profit, chair production and man-hours use; eight variables: chair, table, U1, E1, U2, E2, U3, E3; and five constraints: wood availability, man-hours availability, profit goal, chair production goal and labor hours' usage.

Once the GP model is developed, you are ready to solve it using WinQSB. To solve this problem, open WinQSB and select the **Goal Programming** module. On the toolbar, click on **File** and then **New Problem**. A menu will appear as shown in Figure 3.1.

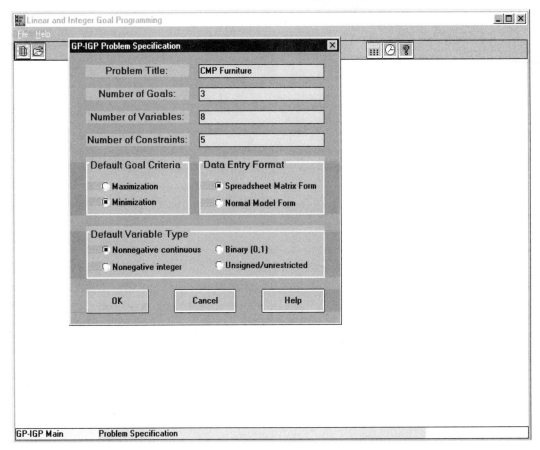

Figure 3.1

Enter the **Problem Title**, **Number of Goals**, **Number of Variables**, **Number of Constraints**, and then select under **Default Goal Criteria**: **Minimization**, **under Default Variable Type: Nonnegative continuous** (we will discuss other selections later in the manual). Now you have the option of entering data in either **Spreadsheet Matrix Form** or **Normal Model Form**. My recommendation is that you start with first option

(See Figure 3.1). Click OK and you will see a screen as shown in Figure 3.2 and you are then ready to input data into the spreadsheet form.

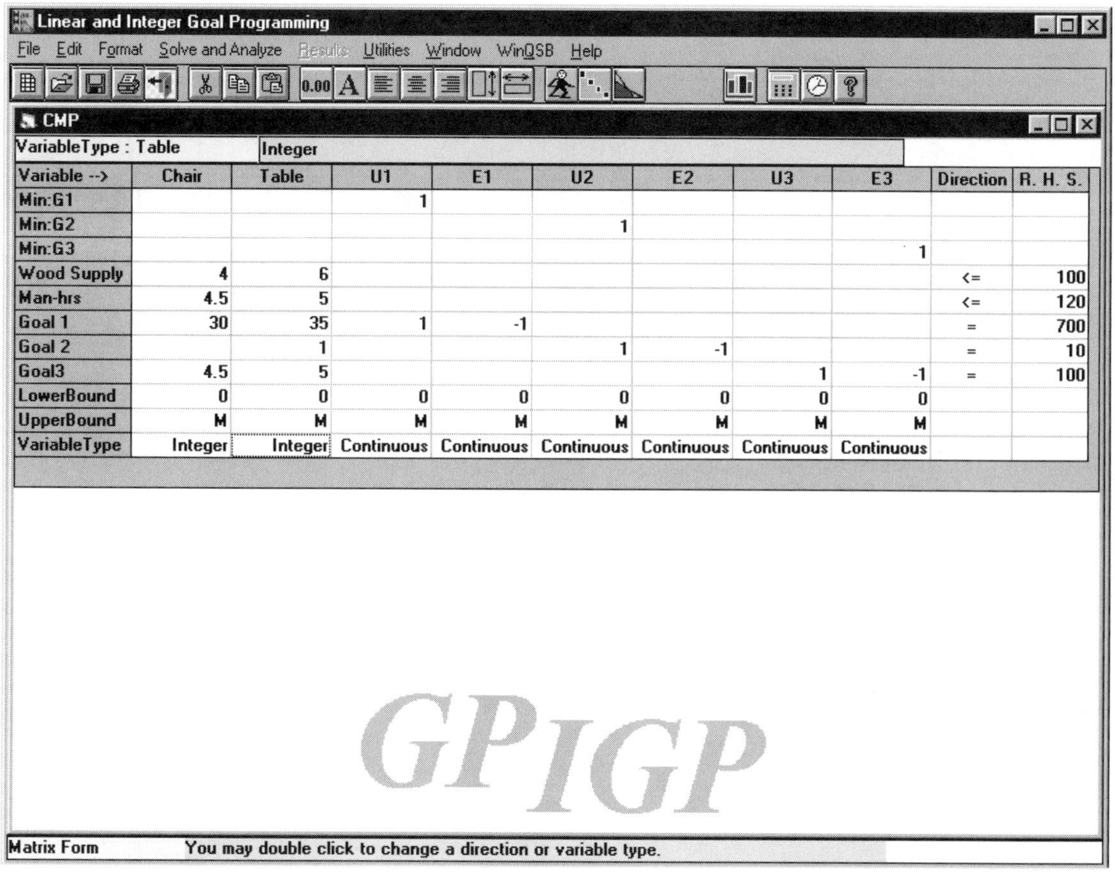

Linear and Integer Goal Programming

File   Edit   Format   Solve and Analyze   Results   Utilities   Window   WinQSB   Help

CMP

VariableType : Table   Integer

Variable -->	Chair	Table	U1	E1	U2	E2	U3	E3	Direction	R. H. S.
Min:G1			1							
Min:G2					1					
Min:G3								1		
Wood Supply	4	6							<=	100
Man-hrs	4.5	5							<=	120
Goal 1	30	35	1	-1					=	700
Goal 2		1			1	-1			=	10
Goal3	4.5	5					1	-1	=	100
LowerBound	0	0	0	0	0	0	0	0		
UpperBound	M	M	M	M	M	M	M	M		
VariableType	Integer	Integer	Continuous	Continuous	Continuous	Continuous	Continuous	Continuous		

GPIGP

Matrix Form   You may double click to change a direction or variable type.

Figure 3.2

In the variable row, you will see decision variables as X1 and X2, and C1 and C2 represent the two constraints (these are default values). You can change all these by clicking "Edit" on the Toolbar. Figure 3.2 shows the edited variable and constraint names. Now you can enter data just like in the CMP LP model. You can enter a number and Tab to next cell for number entry (just like in Microsoft EXCEL).

Once you have completed the data entry, click on **Solve and Analyze** on the toolbar. Here you will get several options for solving the GP problem: **Solve the Problem** (this option will give you final solution using the simplex algorithm, including sensitivity analysis), **Solve and Display Steps** (this option will display step (tableau) by step (tableau) the simplex algorithm output), and **Graphic Method** (the graphical display of solution for two decision variables problem only). The solution to our problem is shown in Figure 3.3, and the sensitivity analysis in Figure 3.4

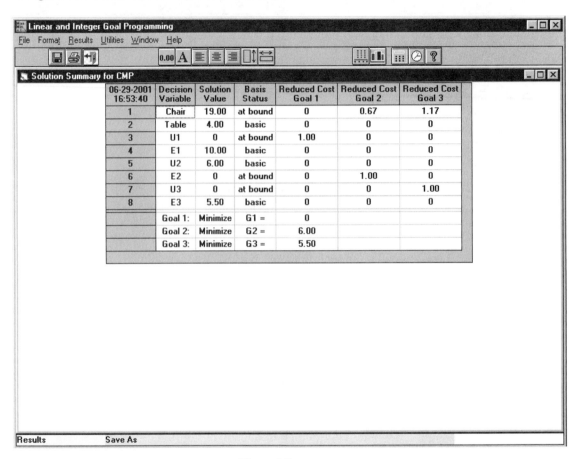

06-29-2001 16:53:40	Decision Variable	Solution Value	Basis Status	Reduced Cost Goal 1	Reduced Cost Goal 2	Reduced Cost Goal 3
1	Chair	19.00	at bound	0	0.67	1.17
2	Table	4.00	basic	0	0	0
3	U1	0	at bound	1.00	0	0
4	E1	10.00	basic	0	0	0
5	U2	6.00	basic	0	0	0
6	E2	0	at bound	0	1.00	0
7	U3	0	at bound	0	0	1.00
8	E3	5.50	basic	0	0	0
	Goal 1:	Minimize	G1 =	0		
	Goal 2:	Minimize	G2 =	6.00		
	Goal 3:	Minimize	G3 =	5.50		

Figure 3.3

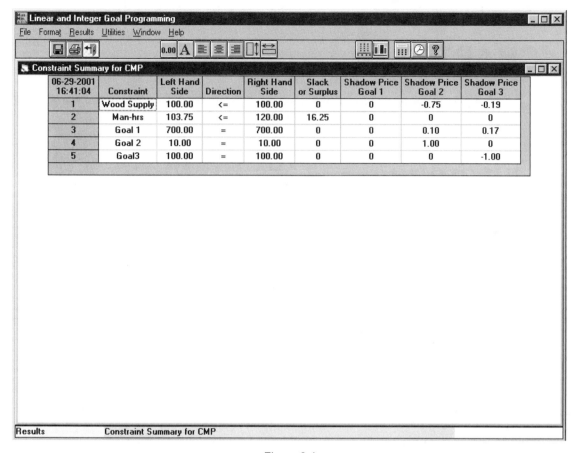

Figure 3.4

CHAPTER 4

Quadratic Programming (QP) and Integer Quadratic Programming (IQP)

This programming module solves quadratic programming (QP) and integer quadratic programming (IQP) problems. A QP or IQP problem differs from a linear programming problem in that the objective function is of second order. There are limited numbers of linear constraints. One can have non-negative continuous decision variables, integer decision variables, binary decision variables, or unsigned/unrestricted decision variables. This module employs simplex and graphic (two decision variables only) methods for the QP problem. For IQP problems, it uses a branch-and-bound algorithm to solve the problem.

CMP furniture produces chairs and tables. Demand for the products depends on the price of the products. The demand for chairs (X_1) and for tables (X_2) is defined as

$$X_1 = 4500 - 10P_1$$
$$X_2 = 7600 - 20P_2$$

Where P_1 and P_2 are the prices for chairs and tables respectively.

The cost of making a chair is $40 and the cost of producing a table is $70. This makes the objective function:

Maximize profit: $(P_1-40) X1 + (P_2-70) X2$

Furniture production has the following resource constraints: wood availability, manufacturing man-hours and finishing shop man-hours as shown below:

$3X_1 + 4X_2 \le$ 7000 board feet
$4X_1 + 6X_2 \le 10,000$ man-hours for manufacturing
$X_1 + 2X_2 \le$ 5000 man-hours for finishing

By making the proper substitution for X_1 and X_2 in terms of P_1 and P_2, you get the following quadratic model:

Maximize profit: $4900P_1 -10P_1{}^\wedge2 + 9000P_2- 20P_2{}^\wedge2 - 712000$

s.t.

$-30P_1 -80P_2 \le -36900$
$-40P_1-120P_2 \le -53600$
$-10P_1-40P_2 \le -14700$

P_1, P_2 are non-negative.

To solve this problem, open WinQSB, select the **Quadratic Programming** module, and then click on **File** and then **New Problem** (Figure 4.1). Enter CMP FURNITURE for the **Problem Title**. Enter two for the **Number of Variables**. The **Number of Constraints** is equal to three. The **Objective Criterion** is Maximization. The **Default Variable Type** is Nonnegative continuous, and the **Data Entry Format** will be in Normal Model Form. Now click **OK**. Enter the data as shown in Figure 4.2. Here the variable names are edited from the default X_1 and X_2 to P_1 and P_2 by using the **Edit** function on the toolbar and then clicking on **Variable Names**. Note that the constant -712000 is omitted from the objective function. Click on **Solve and Analyze**, and select **Solve the Problem**. The combined report/solution will be displayed as shown in Figure 4.3.

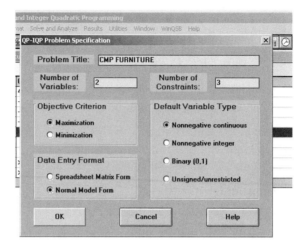

Figure 4. 1

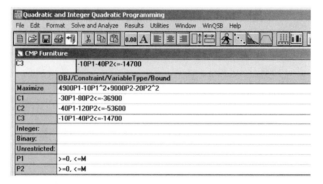

Figure 4.2

08:01:26			Friday	March	29	2002		
	Decision Variable	Solution Value	Unit Cost or Profit c(i)	Total Contribution	Dual Slack	Basis Status	Allowable Min. c(i)	Allowable Max. c(i)
1	P1	329.51	4,900.00	1,614,609.88	0	basic	-3,543.75	5,425.00
2	P2	337.68	9,000.00	3,039,146.25	0	basic	7,600.00	14,775.00
3	P1	* P1	-10.00	-1,085,783.00				
4	P2	* P2	-20.00	-2,280,595.00				
	Objective	Function	(Max.) =	1,287,377.88				
	Constraint	Left Hand Side	Direction	Right Hand Side	Slack or Surplus	Shadow Price	Allowable Min. RHS	Allowable Max. RHS
1	C1	-36,900.00	<=	-36,900.00	0	56.34	-M	-36,830.00
2	C2	-53,702.44	<=	-53,600.00	102.44	0	-53,702.44	M
3	C3	-16,802.44	<=	-14,700.00	2,102.44	0	-16,802.44	M

Figure 4.3

From the above solution, we see that CMP should produce 329.51 chairs and 337.68 tables. We can treat the same problem as an integer quadratic programming problem by redefining the variable types to be integer, nonnegative variables. Click on **Window** on the toolbar, select **CMP Furniture**, and you will see your original data (Figure 4.2). Now enter P_1, P_2 in the 'Integer' row. Here we are restricting the decision variables to be integer only (Figure 4.4). Now click **Solve and Analyze** on the toolbar and WinQSB will display the integer solution for CMP, 326 chairs and 339 tables to be produced (Figure 4.5).

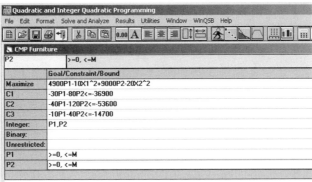

Figure 4.4

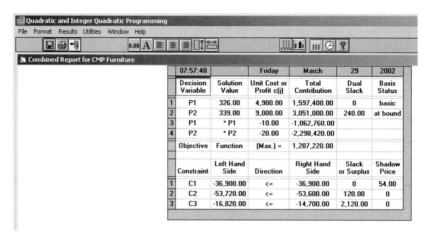

Figure 4.5

CHAPTER **5**

Network Modeling

This programming module, Network Modeling, solves network problems including capacitated network (transshipment), transportation, assignment, shortest path, maximal flow, minimal spanning tree and traveling salesperson problems. A network consists of nodes and connections (arcs/links). Each node may have a capacity (in case of the network flow and transportation problems). If there is a connection between two nodes, there may be a cost, profit, distance, or flow capacity associated with the connection. Based on the nature of the problem, NET solves the link or shipment to optimize the specific objective function.

1. TRANSPORTATION PROBLEM

The transportation problem deals with the distribution of goods from several supply sources to several demand locations. Here the objective is to ship the goods from supply sources to demand locations at the lowest total cost. The transportation problem could be balanced (the supplies and demands are equal) or could be unbalanced (supplies and demand do not match).

Let's look at the CMP furniture manufacturer's dilemma. It has production facilities in Nashville and Atlanta and its markets are in New York, Miami, and Dallas. Production capacity at the Nashville plant is 300 units and Atlanta has a capacity of 500 units. The demand at New York, Miami, and Dallas are 150, 300, and 350 units, respectively.

The cost of shipping per unit from Nashville to New York, Miami, and Dallas is $10, $12, and $9 respectively. The unit shipping cost from Atlanta to New York, Miami, and Dallas is $7, $10, and $14 respectively. CMP needs to decide how many of these units need to be shipped from Nashville and Atlanta to New York, Miami, and Dallas at the lowest total cost. This is a typical transportation problem.

To solve this problem, in Windows click on Start, Program, WinQSB, **Network Modeling**. You will see the menu as shown in Figure 5.1. Select problem type Transportation, objective criterion Minimization, Spreadsheet Matrix Form for data entry, problem title CMP, Number of sources 2, and number of destination 3. Now left click the mouse button. You will see the input form. You can edit the "From" and "To" by clicking on edit on the toolbar and typing in Nashville and Atlanta for "From" and New York, Miami and Dallas for "To." Enter appropriate unit shipment cost for "From" to "To," and available supplies and demands at appropriate supply sources and demand points. (See Figure 5.2).

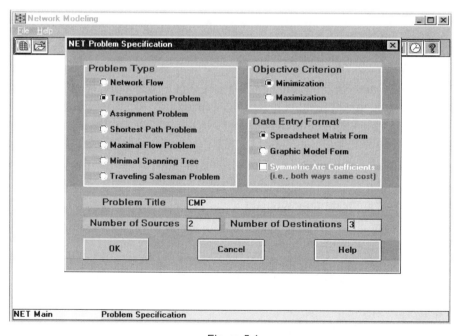

Figure 5.1

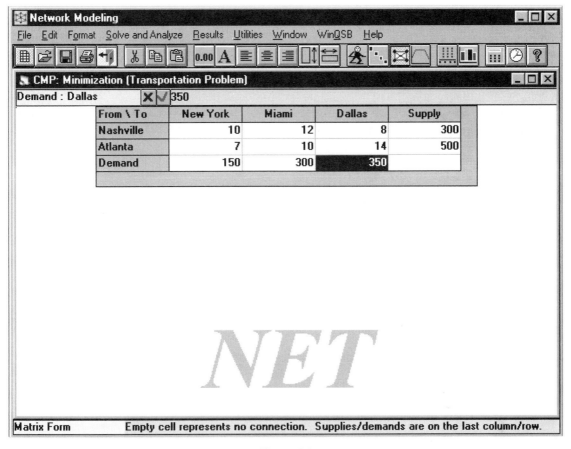

Figure 5.2

Now left click the mouse button on Solve and Analyze and click on Solve Option on the popup menu. You will see the solution output (Figure 5.3).

Optimal solution for this problem is from Nashville ship 300 units to Dallas, and from Atlanta ship 150 units to New York, 300 units to Miami and 50 units to Dallas at the total cost of $7150.

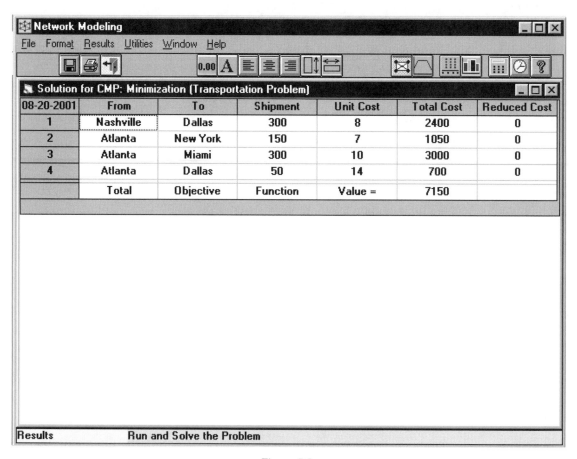

Figure 5.3

If you want to see a graphical representation of this solution, click on "Result," select graphical solution, and you will see the results in graphical representation as shown in Figure 5.4.

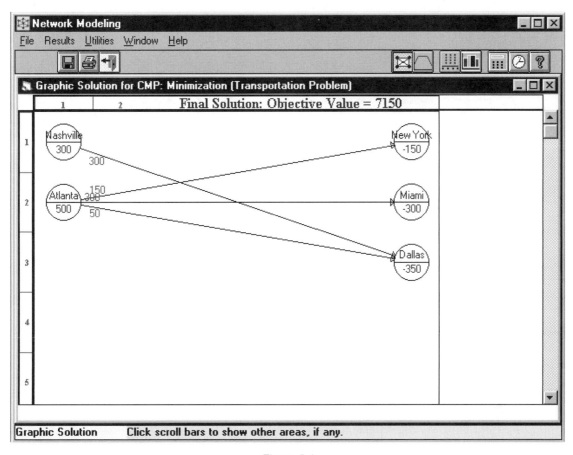

Figure 5.4

2. AN ASSIGNMENT PROBLEM

CMP has three workers, Paul, Tim, and Janet for designing chairs, tables, and a new product. Paul takes 4 days to design a chair, 4 days to design a table and 3 days to design the new product. Tim takes 8 days, 7 days and 6 days to design a chair, table, or new product, respectively, whereas Janet takes 2 days to design a chair, 3 days to design a table and 1 day to design the new product. CMP's owner wants to design a chair, a table, and the new product in the least amount of total person-days. Who should be assigned to design the chair, table, and the new product? This is an assignment problem. From the WinQSB menus, select the Network Modeling option. You will see a menu as shown in Figure 5.5.

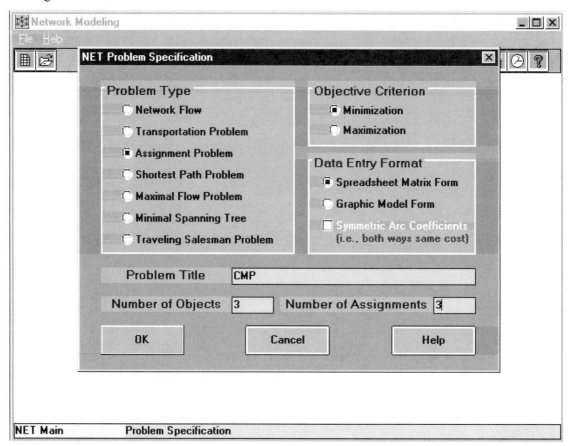

Figure 5.5

Select the **Problem Type**: Assignment Problem; **Objective Criterion**: Minimization; **Data Entry Format**: Spreadsheet Matrix Form; **Problem Title**: type in CMP; **Number of Objects** (chair, table and new product) equal to 3; and **Number of Assignments** (Paul, Tim and Janet) equal to 3. Click on OK. Now you will see an input window as shown in Figure 5.6. Edit the names of object and assignment by clicking on edit, and node names to display Chair Design, Table Design, New Product, Paul, Tim, Janet.

Left click on Solve and Analyze and select solve the problem, and you will see results as shown in Figure 5.7. The assignment solution consists of chair design to Janet, table design to Paul and new product design to Tim, with the total lowest time of 12 person-days.

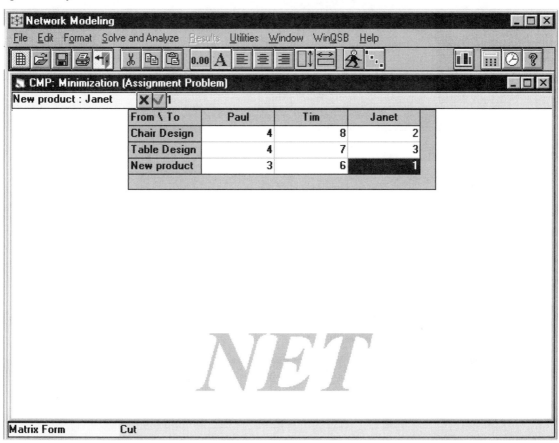

Figure 5.6

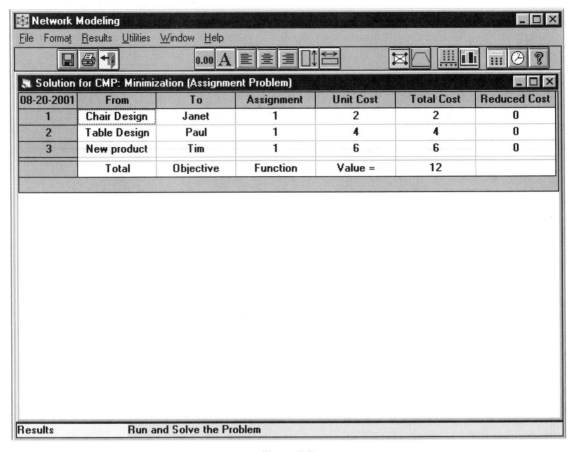

Figure 5.7

3. SHORTEST PATH PROBLEM.

Let say CMP's trucks can only travel between CMP headquarters and its manufacturing plants in Nashville and Atlanta and its markets in Dallas, Miami and New York as shown in Figure 5.8. The owner wants to know the shortest distance from headquarters to Miami. One would use the shortest path model to find the answer. Select **Network Modeling** from the WinQSB menu, and then select **Shortest Path Problem** from the Problem Type option. Objective Criterion is set to Minimization. Again, select

Spreadsheet Matrix Form. Problem Title is typed in as CMP and number of nodes equals six (Figure 5.9). Click the OK button and you will get the now familiar matrix input form. Go to edit on toolbar, and select node name option to type in node names i.e. CMP, Nashville,…, Miami. Now the enter distance between the nodes (Figure 5.10). Go to the Solve and Analyze option on toolbar and left click the mouse button. Menu as shown in Figure 5.11 will pop open on the screen. In "Click to select a start node," select CMP and on "Click to select an end node," select Miami. Now click on solve and you will see the solution on your screen as shown in Figure 5.12. Here the shortest route from CMP headquarters to Miami is via Atlanta and the total distance is 1020 miles. You also see the distance from CMP headquarters to other cities. If you click on results on the toolbar and select graphic solution, the screen will display the solution as shown in Figure 5.13.

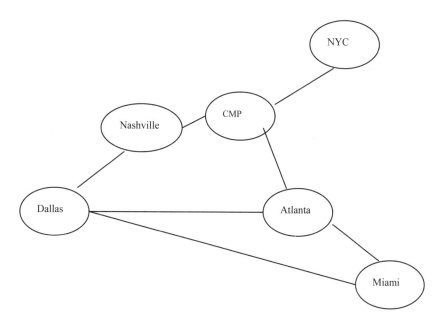

Figure 5.8

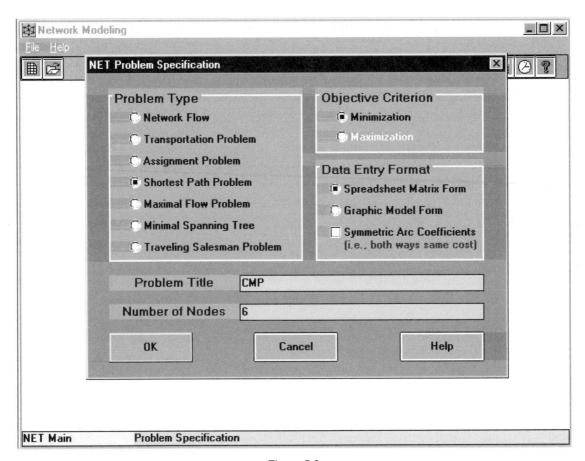

Figure 5.9

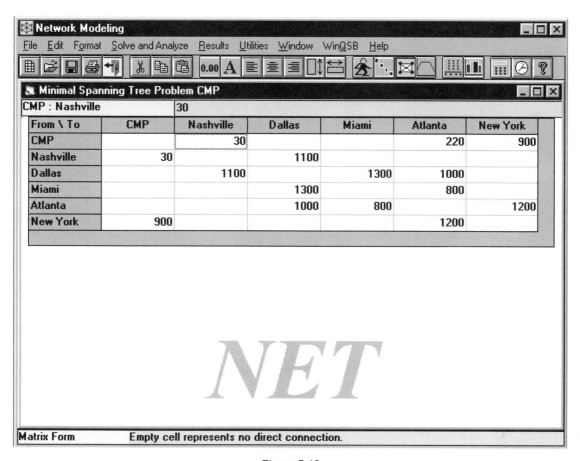

Figure 5.10

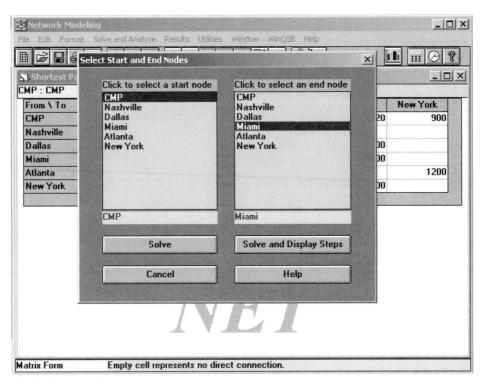

Figure 5.11

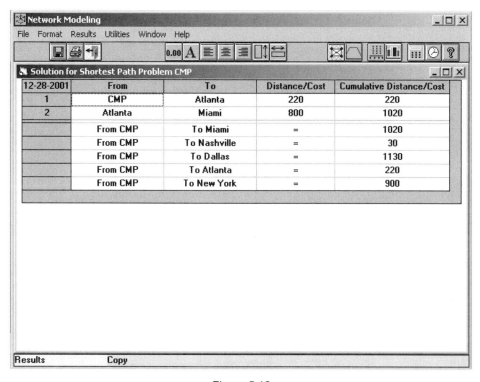

Figure 5.12

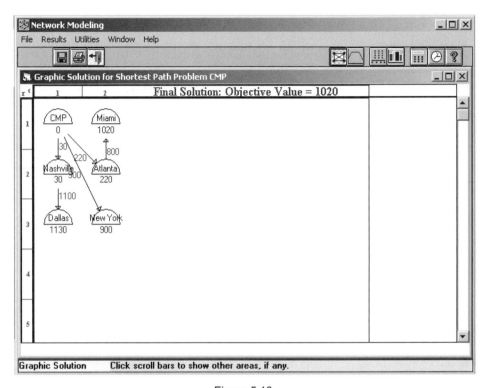

Figure 5.13

4. MAXIMAL FLOW PROBLEM

You are in charge of civilian defense of a city. You need to evacuate the city as quickly as possible. The road map for removing the citizens is shown in Figure 5.14. Capacities of roads in terms of the number of vehicles per minute. In WQSB, select **Network Modeling**. In Problem Type, select **Maximal Flow Problem**. The Objective Criterion is by default Maximization. Again, we will use Spreadsheet Matrix Form for data input. Enter Problem Title: Problem-1 Max Flow, for number of Nodes, enter 6 (there are total of six nodes in this problem). Click OK. See Figure 5.15. Figure 5.16 displays the inputs for this problem. Note that the node names are not replaced here, these are default names. The flow values in appropriate from/to cells are already entered. On the toolbar, click Solve and Analyze, next click on start node "IN" and end node "OUT." Now click on solve (see Figure 5.17).

Figure 5.18 displays the solution. All together one can process 11 cars per minute from this road network. Figure 5.19 displays the graphical solution option from the result button on the toolbar.

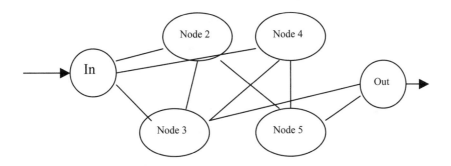

Figure 5.14

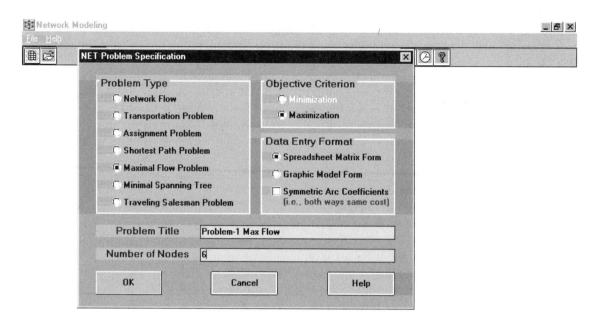

Figure 5.15

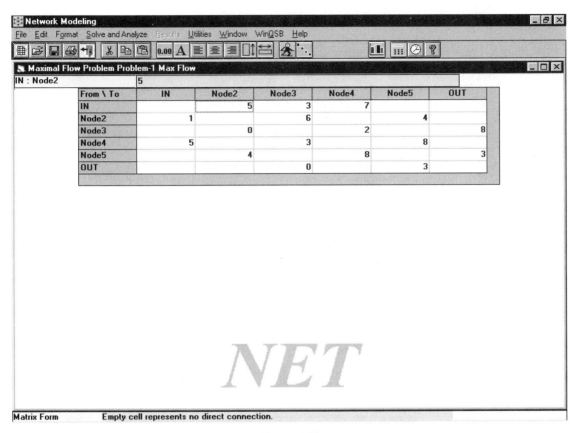

Figure 5.16

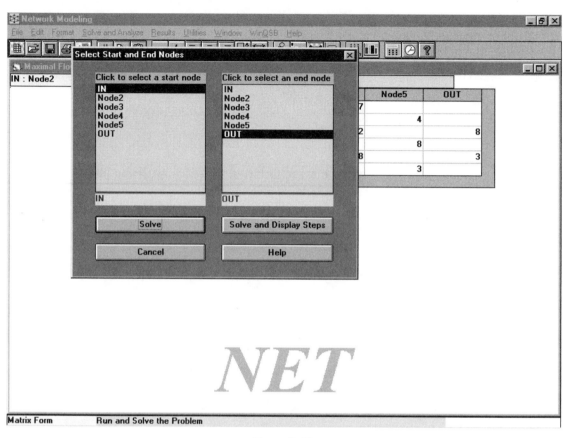

Figure 5.17

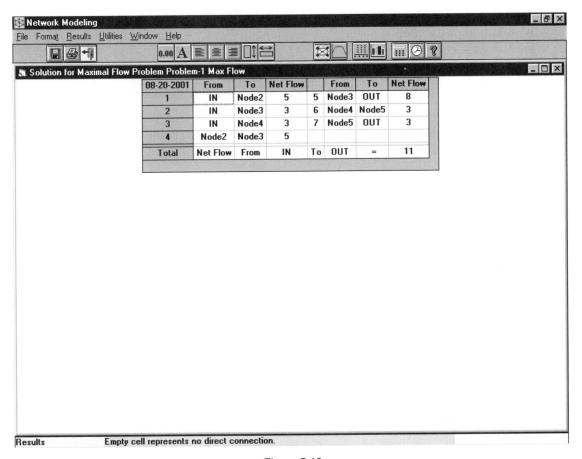

Figure 5.18

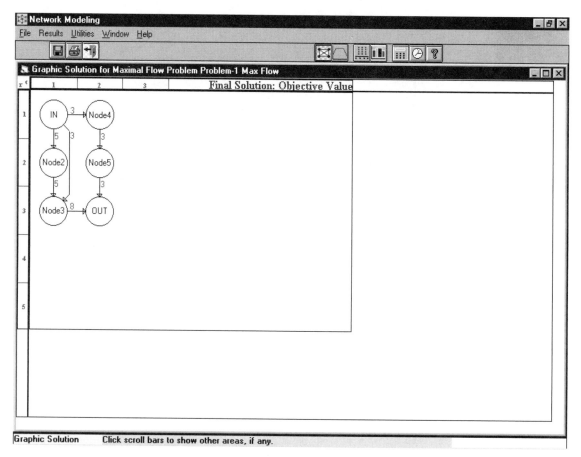

Figure 5.19

5. A MINIMAL SPANNING TREE PROBLEM.

CMP needs to install a sprinkler system in their office. The layout of the office is as shown in Figure 5.20. CMP wants to minimize the total length of pipes to be installed. The minimal spanning tree procedure is to be used here. From the WinQSB menu select **Network Modeling**. In NET Problem Specification select **Minimal Spanning Tree**. The Objective Criterion by default is Minimization (Figure 5.21). Select Spreadsheet Matrix Form. Problem name is CMP Safety. There are a total of nine nodes: Entrance, Lobby, Office, Control Room, Computer Room, Shop 1, Shop 2, Restroom, and Storage.

Click OK. Now you will see the spreadsheet matrix input form. The node names are edited from default to actual names (Figure 5.22). Enter the appropriate distances in the from/to cells. After entering all data, click on the Solve and Analyze button on the toolbar. The next screen will display the solution in terms of sprinkler piping connection between the locations. The total length of pipe is 507 feet (Figure 5.23). The graphical solution option gives you the graphical layout of different nodes and the piping connections between them (Figure 5.24).

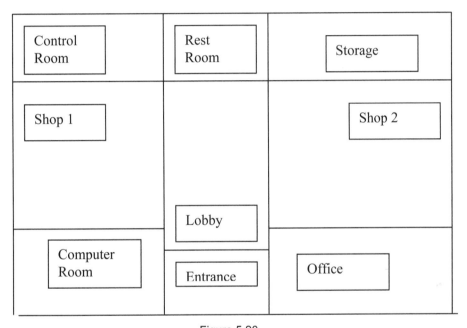

Figure 5.20

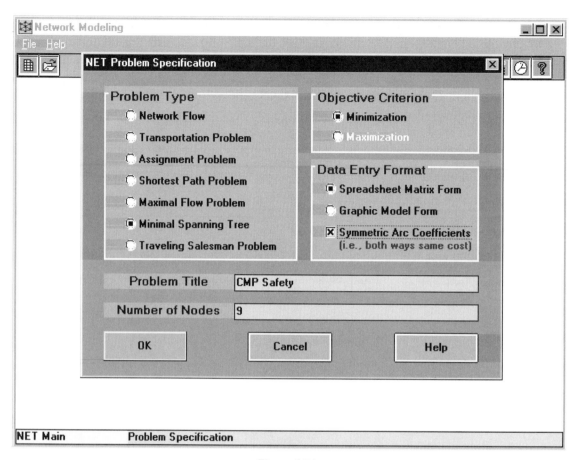

Figure 5.21

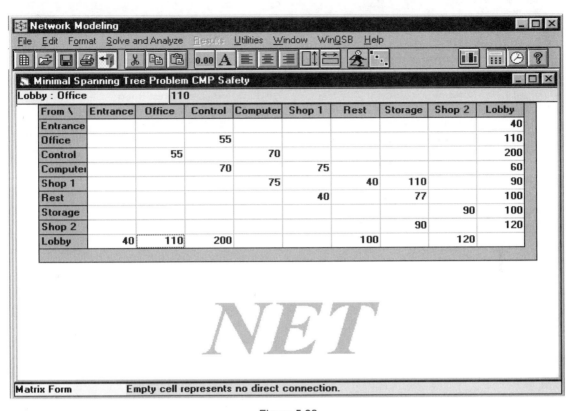

Figure 5.22

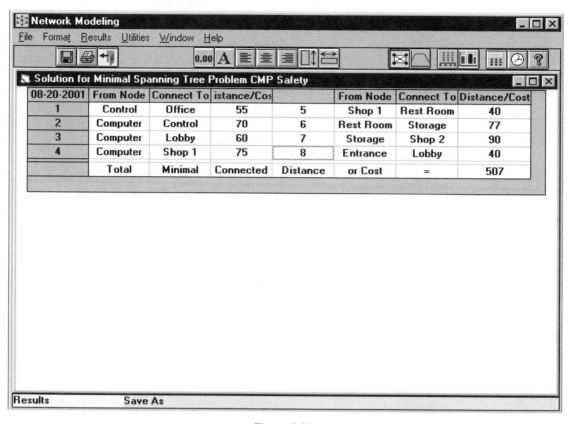

Figure 5.23

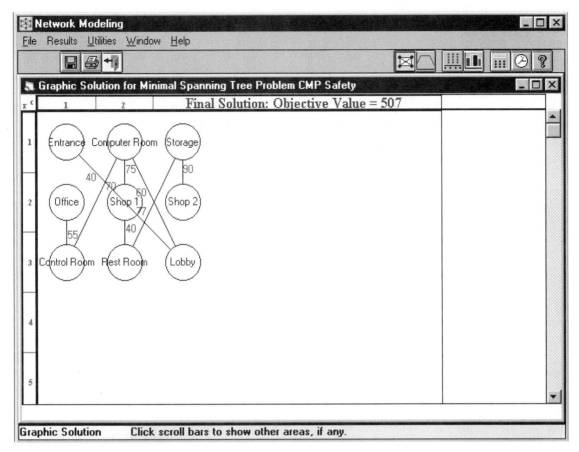

Figure 5.24

6. TRAVELING SALESMAN PROBLEM

CMP has sales representatives visiting between headquarters, the manufacturing facilities, and their customers. A sales representative starts the sales call from headquarters and must visit all the locations without revisiting them and then return to headquarters. This is the classical traveling salesman problem. Figure 5.8 displays the location of all the facilities and their distances.

In WinQSB select **Network Modeling**, then click on **Traveling Salesman Problem**. The Objective Criterion is to minimize the total distance a sales representative has to travel in visiting all of the places. We will use Spreadsheet Matrix form for data input. Enter the name of the problem in the Problem Title space. There are all together six places, hence enter Number of Nodes equal to six. Click OK (see Figure 5.25)

In input form (Figure 5.26), edit the node variables from the Edit menu in the Toolbar and enter the names of nodes. Enter the distance data in appropriate cells. Click on Solve and Analyze. From popup menu, select appropriate solution method (here we have selected Branch and Bound Method) and click Solve (Figure 2.7). The computer will display the solution on the screen (Figure 5.28). The sales person should travel from CMP headquarters to Nashville, from Nashville to Dallas, from Dallas to Miami, from Miami to Atlanta, from Atlanta to New York and from New York to CMP, with a total of 5310 miles traveled. Figure 5.29 shows the graphical solution option output.

Figure 5.25

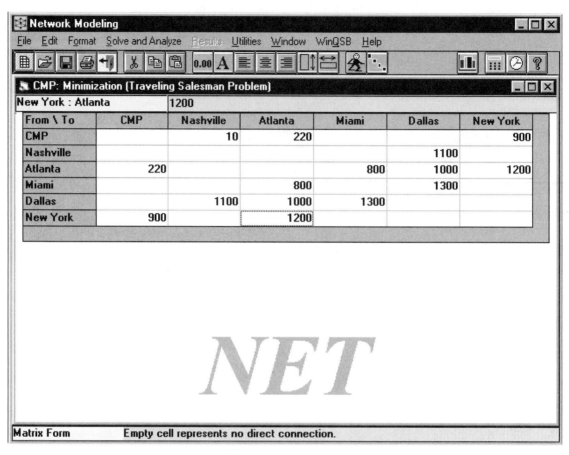

Figure 5.26

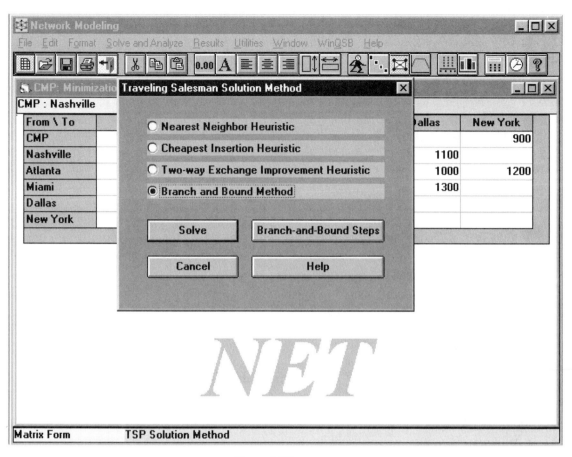

Figure 5.27

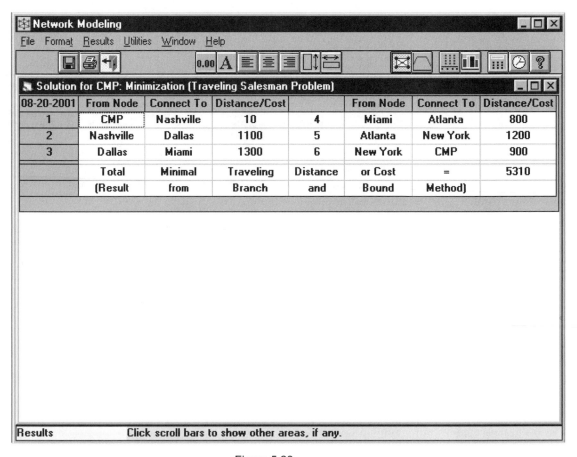

Figure 5.28

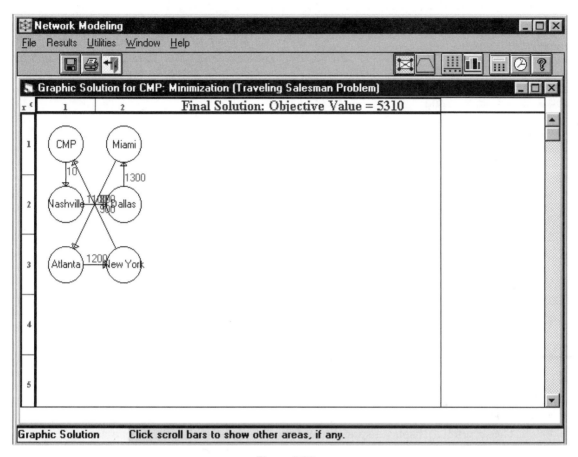

Figure 5.29

7. A NETWORK FLOW (TRANSSHIPMENT) PROBLEM

Figure 5.29 shows a network flow (transshipment) problem. There are two supply points, three transshipment points and two demand points. Supply capacities and demand requirements are shown in the circle and respective shipping costs are shown along the arcs. The decision makers want to ship the goods through transshipment points to demand points at the least possible cost.

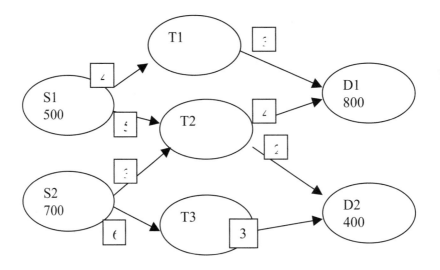

Figure 5.30

Click on WinQSB, and in the popup menu select Network Modeling. From there select Problem Type: Network Flow. The Objective Criterion is Minimization. Select Spreadsheet Matrix Form for data entries. Enter Problem Title: Transshipment Problem. In our problem we have seven nodes, hence enter Number of Nodes equals seven (Figure 5.31). Click OK.

The screen will display a spreadsheet form for inputs with default node names. Click on EDIT on toolbar, select Node names and input appropriate node names, one to be replaced by Supply 1 and so on (Figure 5.32 shows the change of node names) and click OK. Input the data as shown in Figure 5.32. Note that blank cells represent no connections.

Now click on the Solve and Analyze button on the toolbar and select Solve Problem. Solution will be displayed as shown in Figure 5.34. If you want to see another form of the solution, click on result and then select graphical solution. The computer will display the graphical representation of the solution as shown in Figure 5.35.

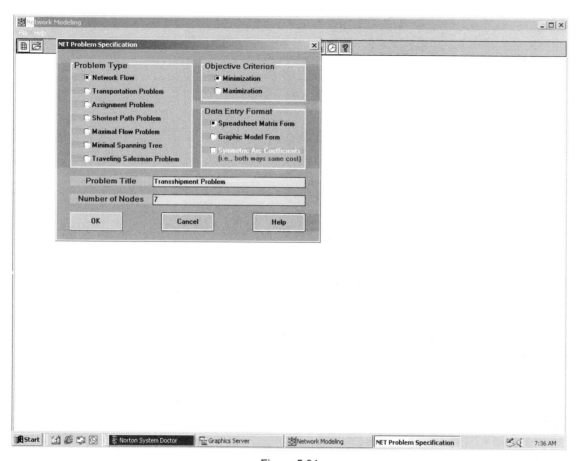

Figure 5.31

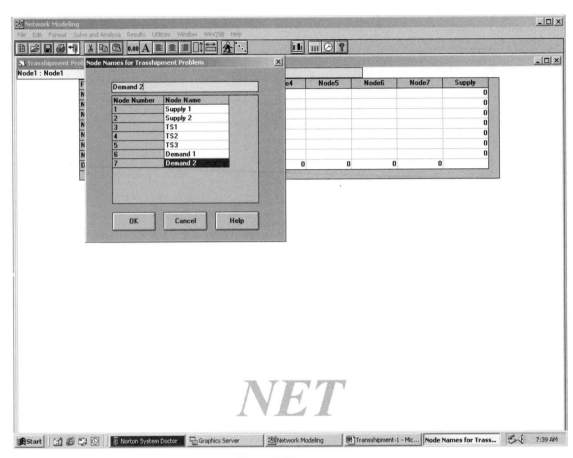

Figure 5.32

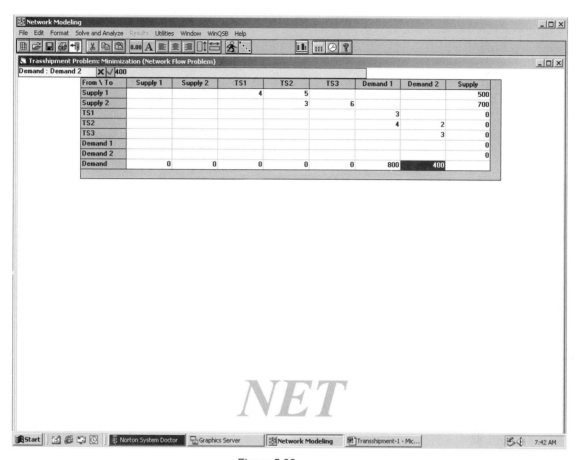

Figure 5.33

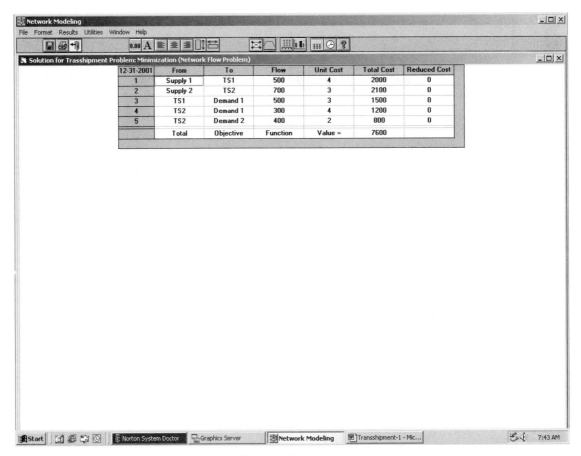

Figure 5.34

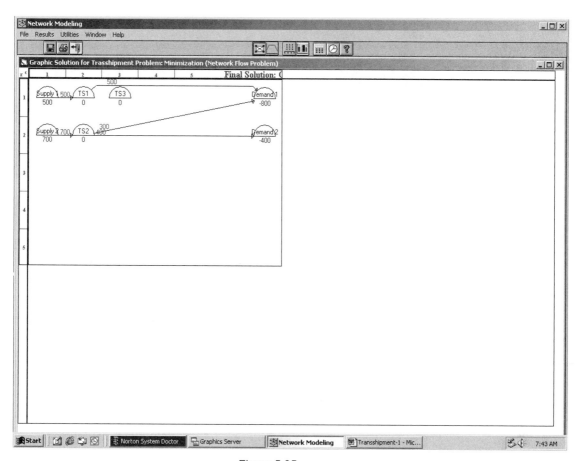

Figure 5.35

CHAPTER **6**

Nonlinear Programming (NLP)

This programming module, Nonlinear Programming (NLP), solves nonlinear programming problems. Like an LP problem, a NLP problem has one objective function and a limited number of constraints. The general form of a nonlinear programming problem is the following:

$$
\begin{aligned}
&\text{Maximize or Minimize} \quad f(x) \\
&\text{Subject to} \qquad\qquad m(x) \leq a \\
&\qquad\qquad\qquad\qquad\; n(x) \geq b \\
&\qquad\qquad\qquad\qquad\; p(x) = c \\
&\qquad\qquad\qquad\qquad\; L \leq x \leq U
\end{aligned}
$$

Where x is a vector of decision variable(s); f is the objective function; m, n, and p are sets of constraint functions; a, b, and c are constant vectors of constraints; L and U are bounds of the variables. NLP's goal is to optimize the objective function while satisfying the constraints, if any. This module solves three types of NLP problems.

1. Unconstrained single variable problem
2. Unconstrained multiple variable problem
3. Constrained problems

Let's look at a sample problem.

Maximize: $-X_1^2 + 2X_1X_2 + X_2^2 - \text{EXP}\,(-X_1 - X_2)$

Subject to: $X_1^2 + X_2^2 = 4$
$X_1 + X_2 \le 1$
$-5 \le X_1 \le 5; -5 \le X_2 \le 5$

To solve the problem open WinQSB and select the Nonlinear Programming module. Click on **File** and then **New Problem** and in the problem specification input, enter the data as shown in Figure 6.1, and click **OK**. Enter the data for the sample problem as displayed in Figure 6.2.   Now click on **Solve and Analyze**, and select **Solve the Problem**. The next screen is for a solution setup. One can leave the default setting or can specify the setup, then click **OK** (Figure 6.3). The solution for the sample problem is shown in the Figure 6.4.   From **Result** on the toolbar, select **Constraint Summary**. Figure 6.5 shows the constraint summary for the sample problem.   For constraint functional analysis, select it from the **Solve and Analyze** option on the toolbar. If one wants to examine the change in value of X1 from -5 to 5, for example, holding X2 constant, select as shown in Figure 6.6 and click on **Table**. The partial output is shown in Figure 6.7. The selection of graphic output results are shown in Figure 6.8. For the objective functional analysis, select that option from **Solve and Analyze** and click on **Objective Functional Analysis**. The input for that is shown in Figure 6.9, and Figure 6.10 shows the graphic output option and Figure 6.11 shows the tabular output.

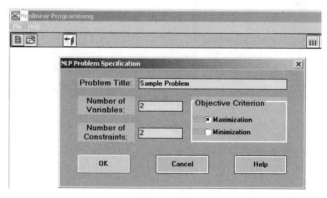

Figure 6.1

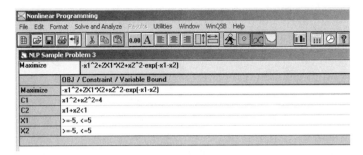

Figure 6.2

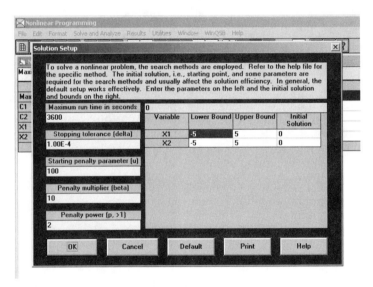

Figure 6.3

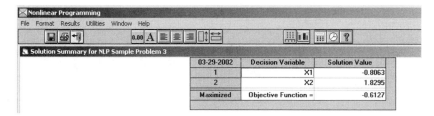

Figure 6.4

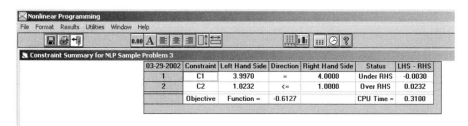

Figure 6.5

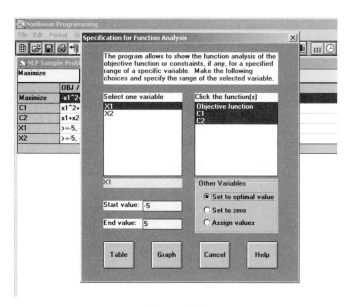

Figure 6. 6

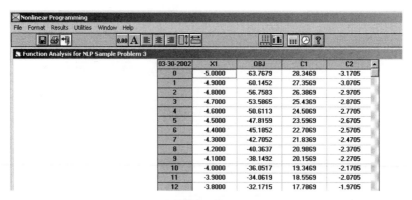

Figure 6. 7

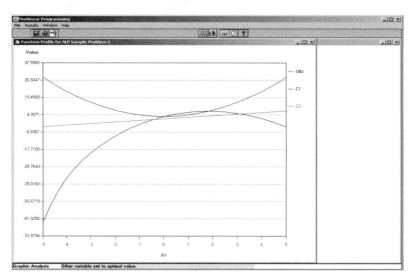

Figure 6. 8

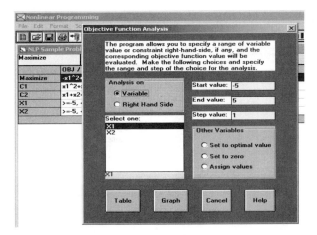

Figure 6. 9

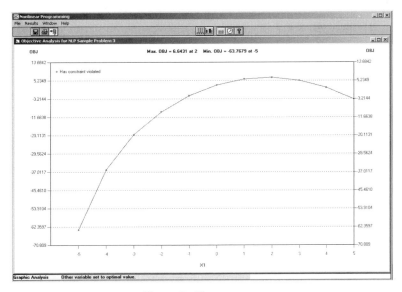

Figure 6. 10

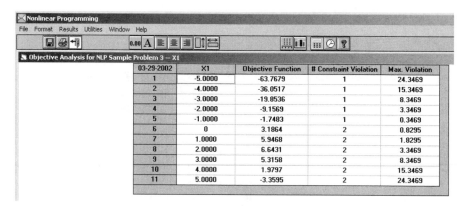

Figure 6. 11

CHAPTER 7

Dynamic Programming (DP)

This programming module, Dynamic Programming (DP), solves dynamic programming problems such as stagecoach, knapsack, and production and inventory scheduling problems. This mathematical technique solves a large problem by decomposing it into a series of small problems that can be solved more easily. Let's look at the shortest route problem we used in chapter 5.

CMP's trucks can only travel between CMP headquarters and its manufacturing plants in Nashville and Atlanta, and its markets in Dallas, Miami and New York as shown in Figure 7.1. The owner wants to know the shortest distance from Nashville to Miami.

To solve this problem open WinQSB and select the Dynamic Programming module. On the toolbar, click on **File**, and then **New Problem**. For the **Problem Type** select stagecoach (shortest route) problem.

The **Problem Title** is CMP and the **Number of Nodes** equals six (Figure 7.2). Click the **OK** button and you will get the matrix input form. Go to **Edit** on the toolbar and select the **Node Names** option to type in node names i.e. CMP, Nashville, Miami etc. Now enter the distance between the nodes (Figure 7.3). Go to the **Solve and Analyze** option on the toolbar, and click on **Solve the Problem**. The menu as shown in Figure 7.4 will pop open on the screen. In **Click to select a start node**, select Nashville and on **Click to select an end node**, select New York. Now click on **Solve** and you will see the solution on your screen as shown in Figure 7.5. Here the shortest route from Nashville to New York is via CMP headquarters and the total distance is 930 miles.

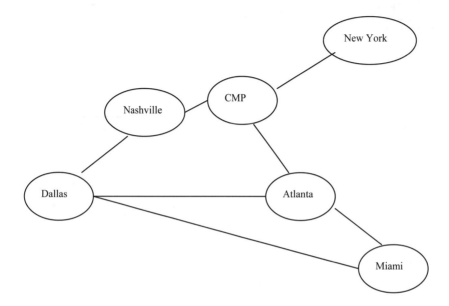

Figure 7.1

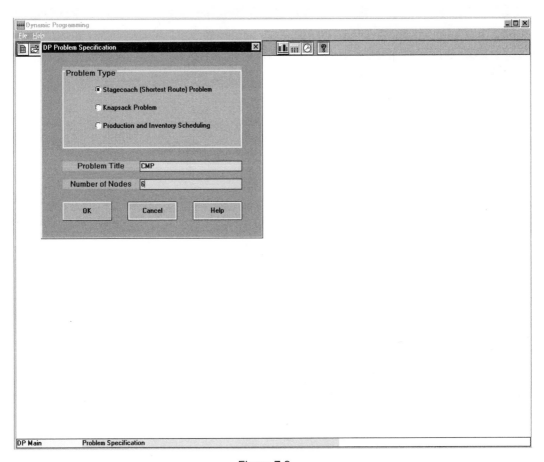

Figure 7.2

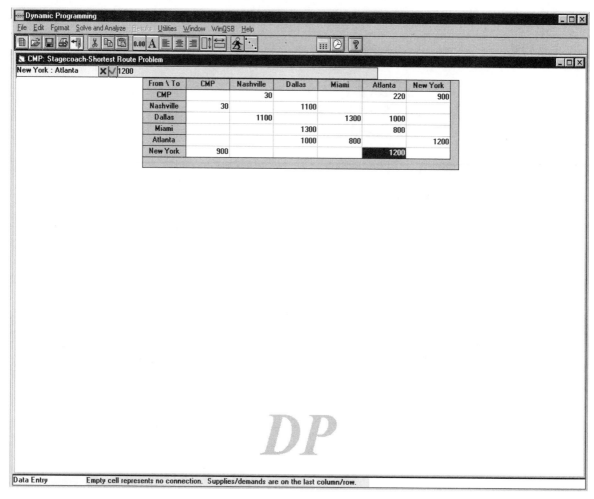

Figure 7.3

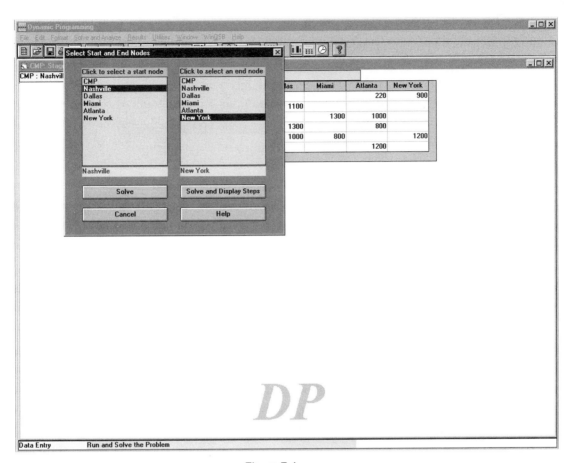

Figure 7.4

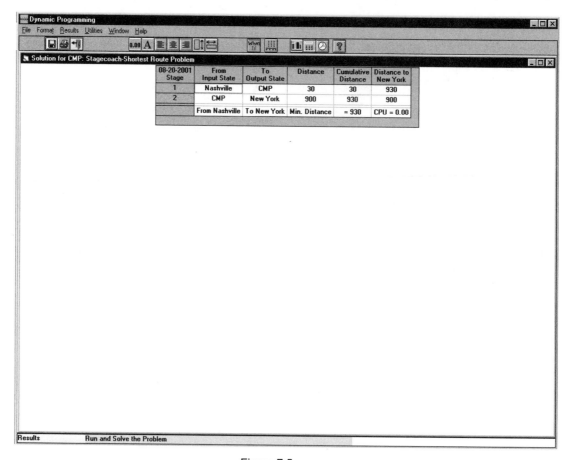

Figure 7.5

KNAPSACK PROBLEM

CMP has to ship 10 chairs of type 1, 4 chairs of type 2, 4 tables, 2 coffee tables, 8 side tables, 2 hutches, 2 sofas and 4 sofa chairs. The total cubic feet of truck space is 35. The cubic feet required for each type of furniture is shown in Table 7.1 below, along with a unit profit contribution per piece. CMP has to decide how many pieces of each type of furniture should be loaded into the truck to maximize total profit without exceeding the truck capacity. This is a typical Knapsack problem.

From WinQSB, select the **Dynamic Programming** module and then click on **File** and **New Problem** and select knapsack problem (Figure 7.6). For **Problem Title**, type in CMP, and for **Number of Items**, type in 8 (there are 8 types of furniture to be shipped). Click on **OK** (see Figure 7.6). In the spreadsheet matrix input form, manually change (as compared to going to Edit on toolbar) the item identification to the appropriate names. Under Units Available, enter the appropriate units available for shipping; under Unit Capacity requirements, enter the appropriate cubic foot space needed for each piece of furniture. In the last column, Return Function, enter the appropriate profit per unit of each type of furniture and symbol of that furniture as in column 2 (see Figure 7.7). Now click on **Solve and Analyze** and you will see the output as shown in Figure 7.8. Here you will be loading 7 Type 1 Chairs, 4 Type 2 Chairs, 4 Tables, 2 Coffee tables, 8 Side Tables, 2 Hutches, 2 Sofas and 4 Sofa chairs into the truck with total profit of $468.

Item (Stage)	Item Identification	Units Available	Unit Capacity Required	Return Function (X: Item ID) (e.g., 50X, 3X+100, 2.15X^2+5)
1	Chair	10	1	10Chair
2	Chair2	4	1	12Chair2
3	Table	4	2	30Table
4	Coffeetable	2	1	10Coffeetable
5	Sidetable	8	0.5	5Sidetable
6	Hutch	2	2	30Hutch
7	Sofa	2	1	25Sofa
8	Sofachair	4	1	15Sofachair
Knapsack	Capacity =	35		

Table 7.1

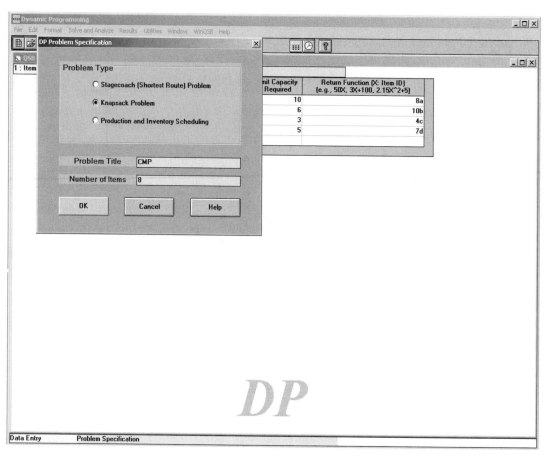

Figure 7.6

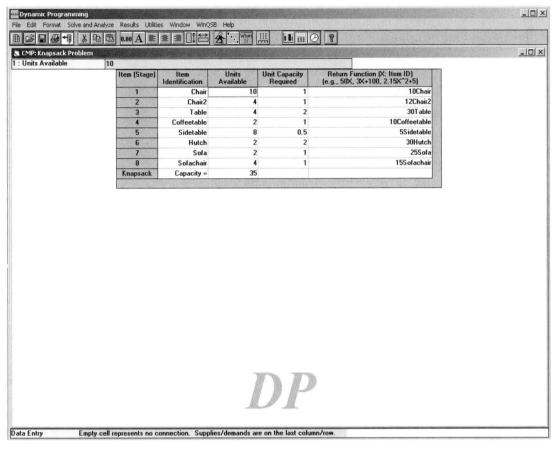

Figure 7.7

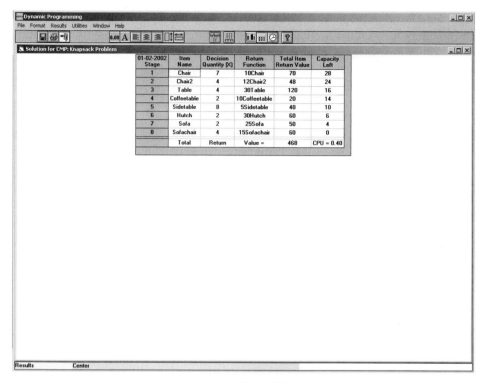

Figure 7.8

PRODUCTION AND *Inventory* SCHEDULING PROBLEM

CMP has to produce chairs for the next 5 months with a demand of 10 in the first month, 8 in the second month, 7 in the third month, 12 in the fourth month and 6 in the fifth month. Production capacity, storage capacity, setup cost, unit production cost, and inventory holding costs are shown below in Table 7.2.

Month	Demand	Production Capacity	Storage Capacity	Production Setup Cost	Unit Production Cost	Holding Unit Cost
1	10	12	10	500	20	30
2	8	12	10	700	20	30
3	7	10	10	700	20	30
4	12	12	15	700	20	30
5	6	12	10	600	20	30

Table 7.2

The initial inventory on hand is equal to two. CMP has to determine the production schedule to minimize the total cost.

From the WinQSB menu, select the Dynamic Programming module. Again click on **File** and **New Problem**. In the DP problem specification menu select the **Production and Inventory Scheduling** option. For **Problem Title**, type in CMP chair, and enter five for the **Number of Periods**. Click **OK** (see Figure 7.9). In the data input matrix, in Period Identification enter Period 1 through Period 5. In the demand column, enter the data from Table 7.2 above. Enter the rest of the data for production capacity, storage capacity, production setup cost, and in the last column for variable cost for each period, enter 20 (unit production cost) times P plus 30 (Holding Unit cost) times H (see Figure 7.10). Now on the toolbar click on **Solve and Analyze**. Figure 7.11 displays the solution to the CMP chair production problem. CMP should produce 11 chairs in period 1, 12 chairs in period 2, no chairs in period 3, 12 chairs in period 4 and 6 chairs in period 5, at a total cost (production, setup cost and holding cost) of $3620.

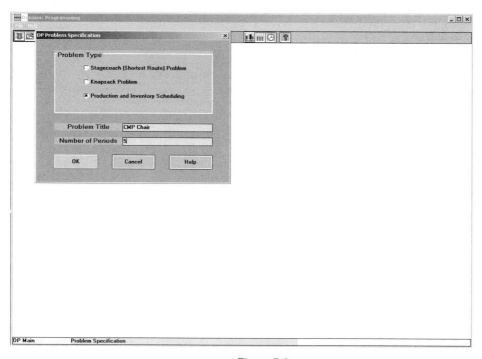

Figure 7.9

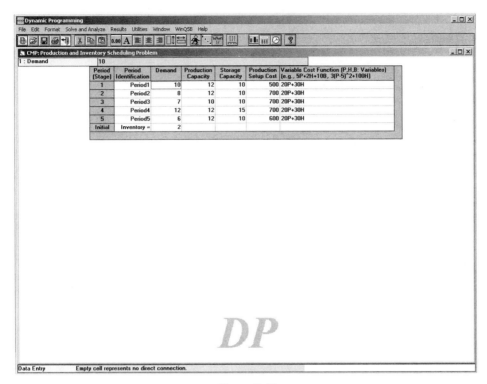

Figure 7.10

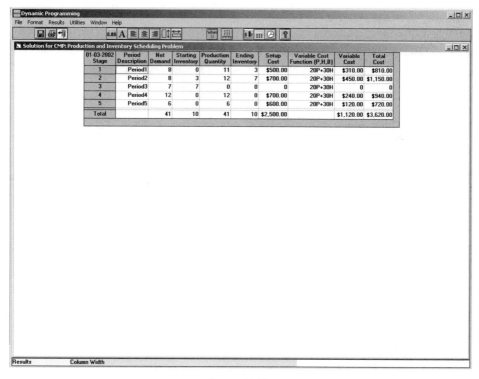

Figure 7.11

CHAPTER 8

Project Scheduling: PERT-CPM

This module, PERT-CPM, creates project analysis for a manager who is managing a project using the Program Evaluation and Review Technique (PERT) or Critical Path Method (CPM). The PERT technique is a stochastic model, whereas CPM is a deterministic model. A project consists of a number of activities and their precedence relations. Once these are determined, PERT-CPM provides the following steps for project management.

1. Performs critical path analysis
2. Performs crashing analysis
3. Performs PERT/COST analysis
4. Performs project cost control for the deterministic activity time project
5. Performs probability analysis for the probability activity time project
6. Displays Gantt chart
7. Identifies multiple critical paths

CMP is developing a new chair design. The development of this project requires 10 activities. These are shown in Table 8.1 with their predecessor relationships and three time estimates.

Activity Number	Activity Name	Immediate Predecessor	Optimistic time	Most likely Time	Pessimistic time
1	A	-	0.5	1	1.5
2	B	A	2	4	6
3	C	A	3	5	7
4	D	B	2	3	4
5	E	B	0.5	1.5	2.5
6	F	C	0.5	1.5	2.5
7	G	C	2	3.5	5
8	H	D, F	2	2.5	3
9	I	E	0.5	1	1.5
10	J	G, I	2	4	6

Table 8.1

In WinQSB, select the **PERT/CPM** module. Click on **File** and select **New Problem**. For **Problem Title** enter CMP; For Number of Activities enter ten; and the **Time Unit** entered should be weeks. Select **Probabilistic PERT** as the **Problem Type**, and the **Data Entry Format** for this problem is a **Spreadsheet**. For **Activity Time Distribution**, select 3-Time estimate. Now click **OK** (see Figure 8.1). The next screen is for data input. Enter the data as shown in Figure 8.2. Now from the toolbar click on **Solve and Analyze**. Figure 8.3 displays the results for this project. It will take thirteen and half weeks to complete the project. The critical activities are activities A, C, G, and J. The critical path is activities A-C-G-J. Here we have only one critical path. Click on **Results** and select **Graphical Activity Analysis,** and it will be displayed as shown in Figure 8.4. Here the earliest start and end times are on the upper half of the node circle and latest start and end times are shown on the bottom half of the node circle for that activity. A dark thick line identifies the critical path. By clicking on **Result** on the toolbar and selecting **Gantt Chart**, the earliest and latest start and end times for each activity are displayed (Figure 8.5). This chart is used for monitoring the progress of each activity.

If one wants to find the probability of completing a project by a certain time, click on **Result**, and select **Perform Probability Analysis** (Figure 8.6). If the probability of completion is less than 26%, than too few resources are allocated for critical activities and if the probability of completion is more than 64%, then too many resources are allocated for critical activities. Here the probability of completing the project was selected to be 13.5 weeks and the probability of completing this project by this time is 50% (Figure 8.7).

Now let's examine another feature of the PERT-CPM module, the time/cost trade off analysis. Suppose CMP wants to complete the project in 11 weeks. CMP came up with a time estimate for the crash time of each activity and the cost of crashing each activity. The normal time estimate came from our PERT analysis and the project manager estimated the normal cost estimate. This information can be found in Table 8.2. To check the feasibility of doing the project in 11 weeks and within a budget of $80,000, let's go back to WinQSB; click on **PERT-CPM**, and click on **File** and **New Problem**. Enter the **Problem Title**, CMP TIME COST; **Number of Activities**, 10; **Time Unit**, week. For **Problem Type** select Deterministic CPM. In **Select CPM Data Field**, select Normal Time, Crash Time, Normal Cost, and Crash Cost. (See Figure 8.8) Again, we will use the spreadsheet as the **Data Entry Format**, and click **OK**. Enter the data as shown in Figure 8.9. In **Solve and Analyze**, select **Perform Crashing Analysis**. If the goal is to complete the project in 11 weeks, Figure 8.10 shows the input requirements. Here for **Desired Completion Time**, enter 11, and then click **OK**. Figure 8.11 shows the results. If CMP wants to know if the allocated amount for the project is $80,000 and how long it will take to finish the project, click on **Result** on the toolbar and select **Perform Crashing Analysis**. Figure 8.12 shows the setup, and Figure 8.13 shows the results.

Activity Name	Immediate Predecessor	Normal Time	Crash Time	Normal Cost	Crash Cost
A		1	0.5	$5	$6
B	A	4	2	7	10
C	A	3	4	10	12
D	B	1.5	3	8	8
E	B	1.5	1.5	4	4
F	C	1	1	4	5
G	C	2.5	2.5	15	20
H	D, F	2.5	2.5	6	6
I	E	1	1	3	3
J	G, J	3	3	9	10

Table 8.2

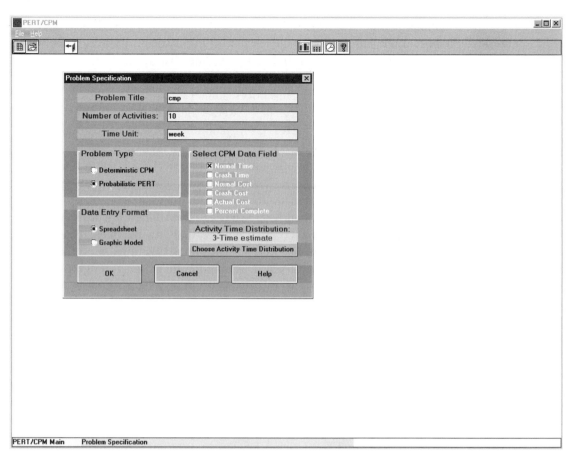

Figure 8.1

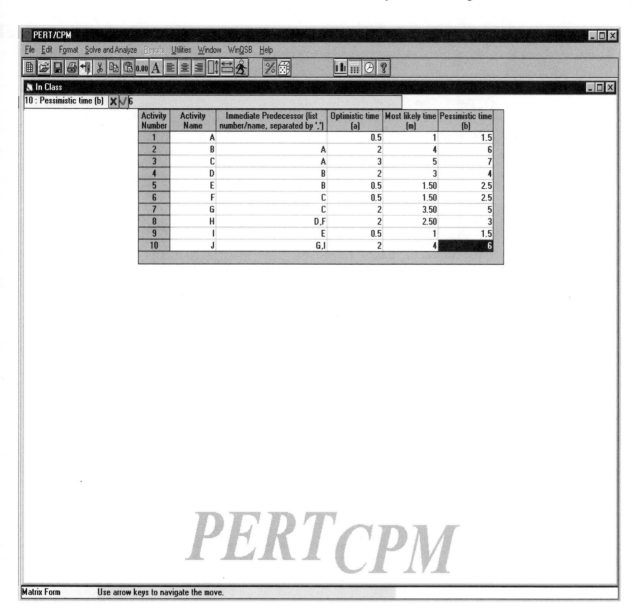

Figure 8.2

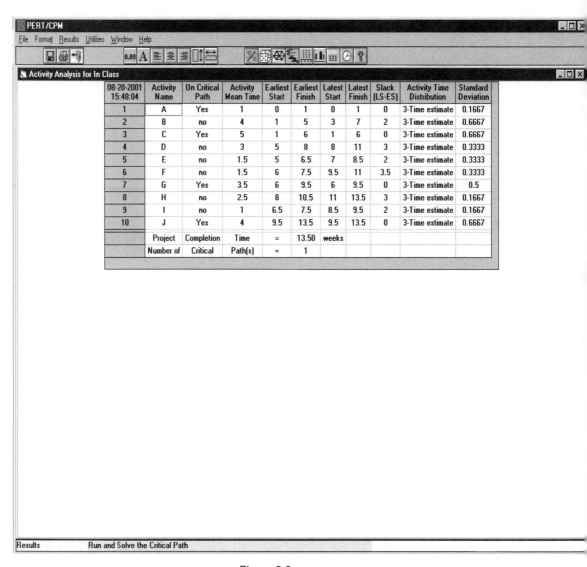

Figure 8.3

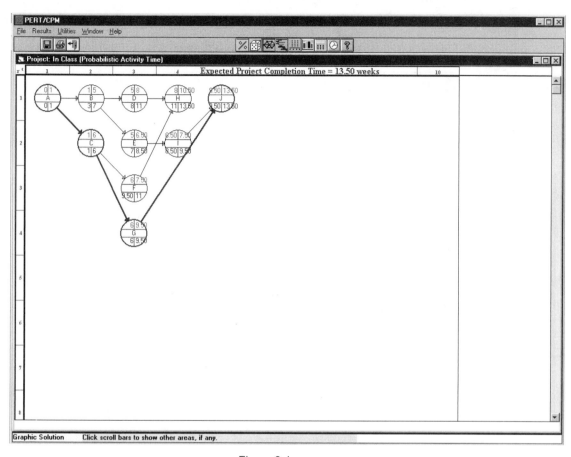

Figure 8.4

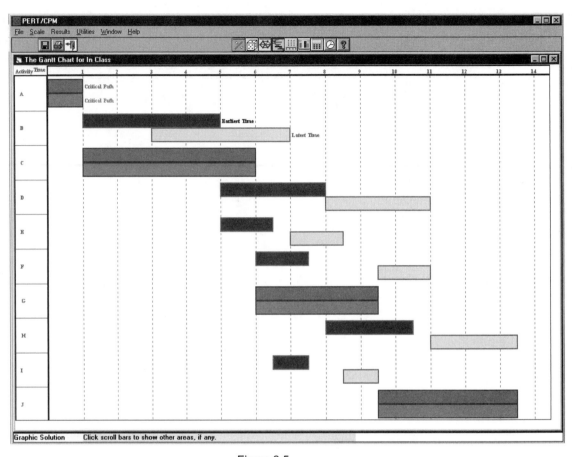

Figure 8.5

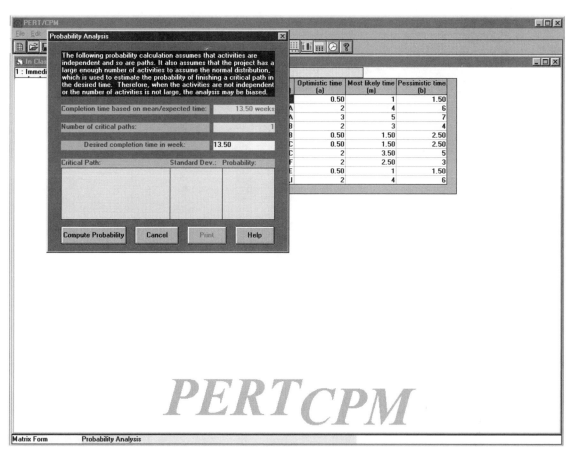

Figure 8.6

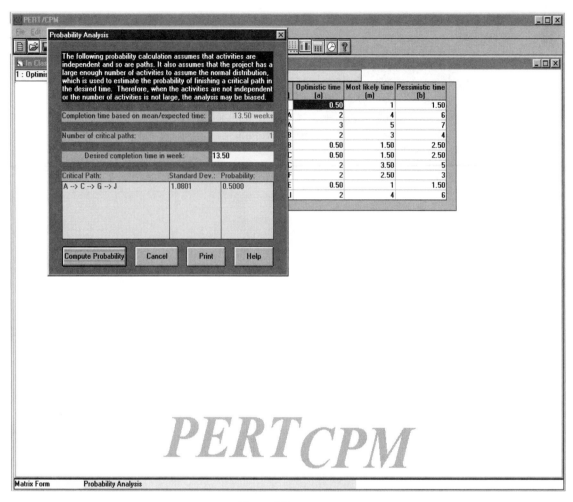

Figure 8.7

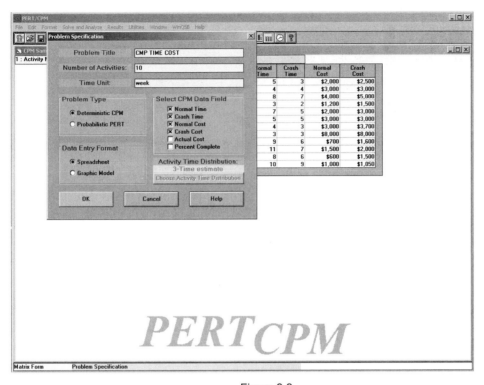

Figure 8.8

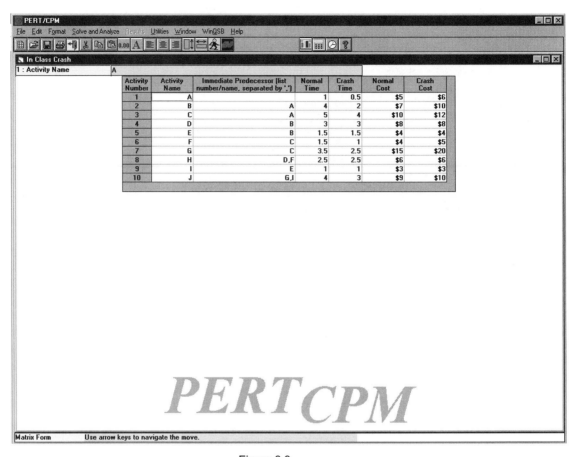

Figure 8.9

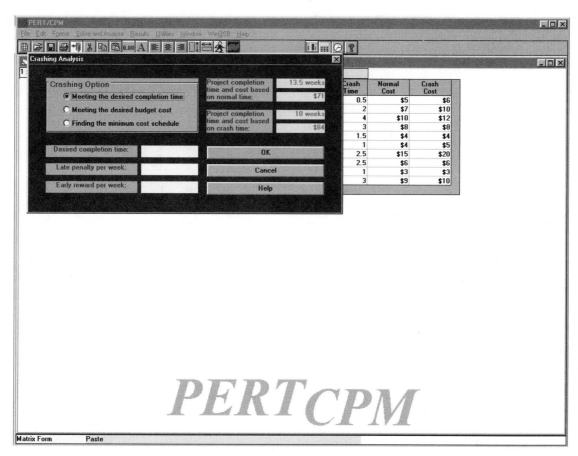

Figure 8.10

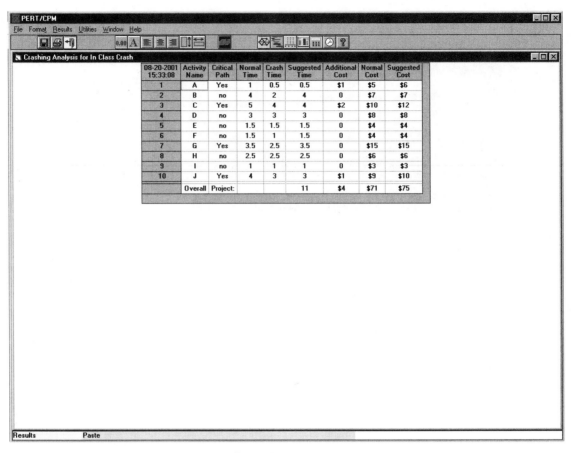

Figure 8.11

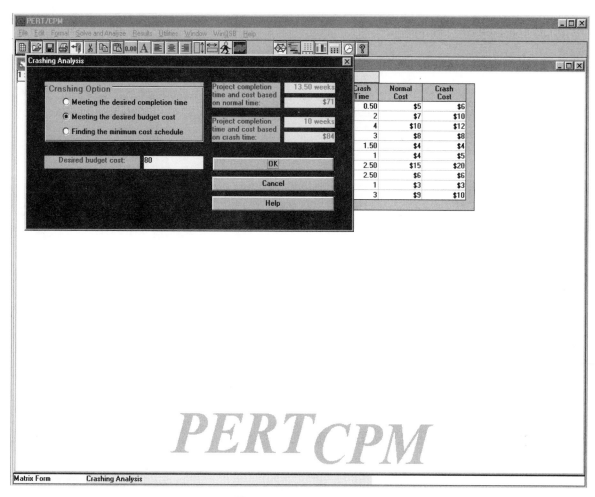

Figure 8.12

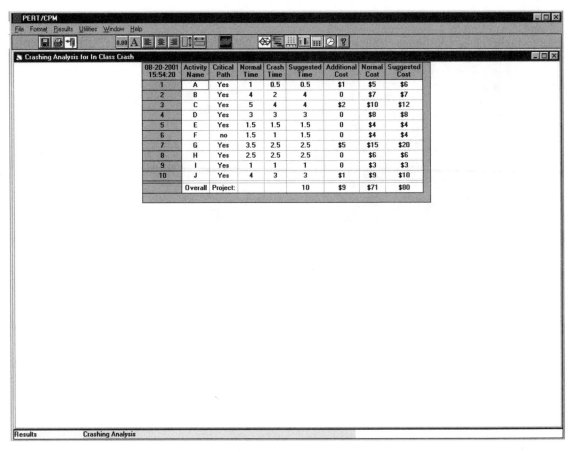

Figure 8.13

CHAPTER 9

Queuing Analysis (QA)

This programming module, Queuing Analysis (QA), examines the behavior of a single-stage queuing (waiting line) problem. A single queuing problem consists of the following elements: a customer population, a queue or waiting line, and a single server or a number of identical servers in parallel. A number of measurements evaluate the performance of a queuing system, such as the average number of customers in the system, the average number of customers in the queue, the average time spent by a customer in the system, the average time spent by a customer in the queue, the probability that the queuing system is idle, and the total cost analysis of a queuing system.

Let us walk through an example problem. CMP has a customer service system. They have one telephone line with an operator dedicated for this purpose. They receive an average of three calls per minute and it takes an average of 15 seconds to help a client. The number of callers that can be put on hold is unlimited. Potentially CMP has unlimited customers, and the cost of the operator is $20.00 per minute. The cost of a customer waiting or being served is estimated to be $50.00 per minute. Click on WinQSB, select the **Queuing Analysis** module, and click on **File** and then **New Problem** (Figure 9.1). For the **Problem Title** enter CMP; **Time Units** enter minutes; select Simple M/M System as the **Entry Format;** and click **OK**. Figure 9.2 shows the data input for the CMP problem. Once you've entered the data, click on **Solve and Analyze** from the toolbar, and select **Solve the Performance**.

Figure 9.3 displays the solution for the CMP problem. Here the total system cost per minute is $170.00, and the customer has to wait for an answer an average of 0.75 minute.

Now CMP wants to explore the possibility of adding one more line and another operator. This problem is classified as an M/M/2 queuing problem. Now click on **Window**, click on **CMP**, and you will see the input menu. Change the **Number of Servers** from one to two, click on **Solve and Analyze,** and select Solve the Performance. (See Figures 9.4 and 9.5) You will see the solution for two identical servers in parallel. Here the average customer waiting time in the queue is reduced to 0.0409 minutes and the total cost of providing the customer support is reduced to $83.6364. If one wants to find the least cost system (i.e. the total number of servers which will minimize the total system cost), click on **Solve and Analyze,** and select **Perform Sensitivity Analysis**. One will see the menu as shown in Figure 9.6. Select **Number of servers** as the **Parameter for Analysis**; for the **Start From** number enter 1; for the **End At** number enter 5, in **Steps** of 1. Now click **OK**. The module will perform a sensitivity analysis of the number of
servers starting at server equal to one and increasing in steps of one all the way to five. The summary output is displayed as shown in Figure 9.7. From the **Total Cost** column, one can see that for CMP the optimal solution for total cost minimization is to have two operators. If you click on **Results** and select **Show Sensitivity Analysis-Graph,** a graphical solution is displayed (Figure 9.8).

Figure 9.1

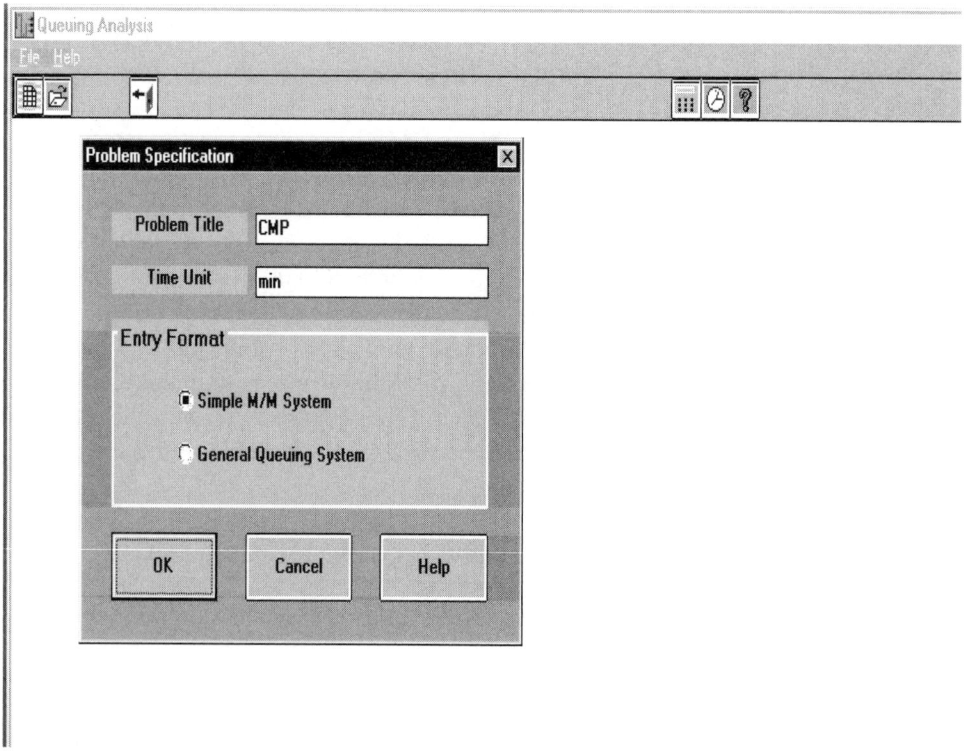

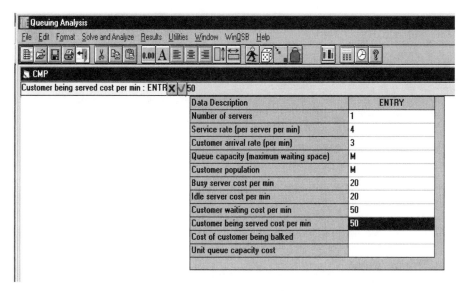

Figure 9.2

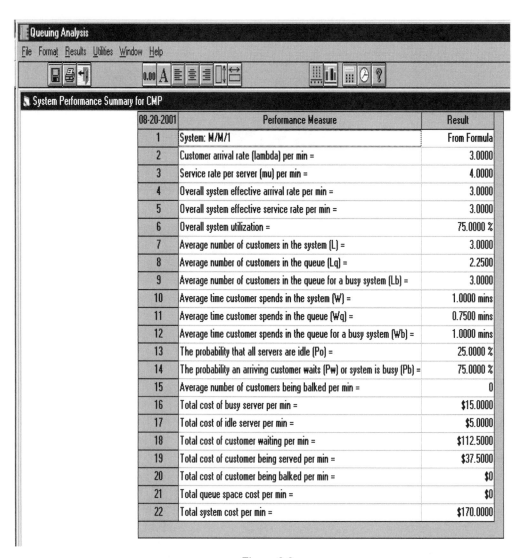

Figure 9.3

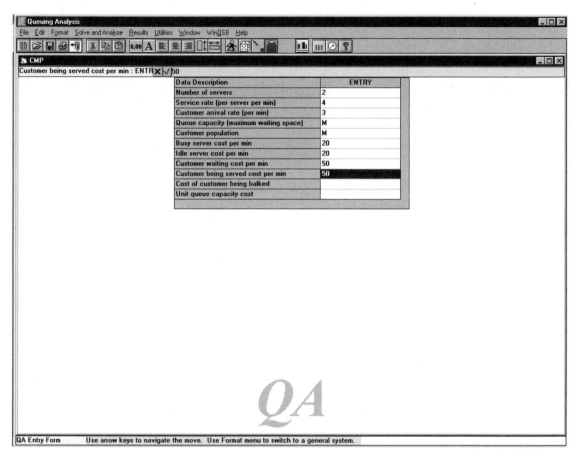

Figure 9.4

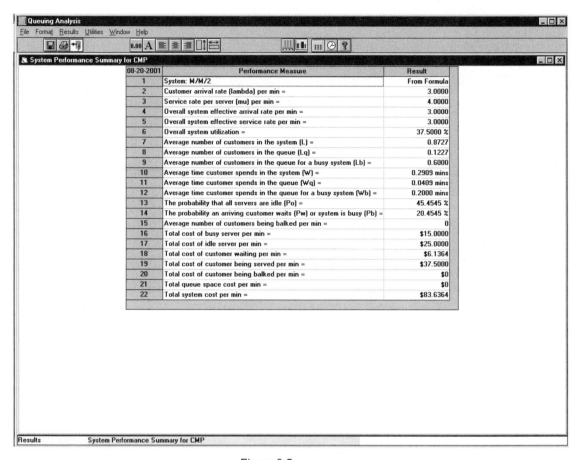

Figure 9.5

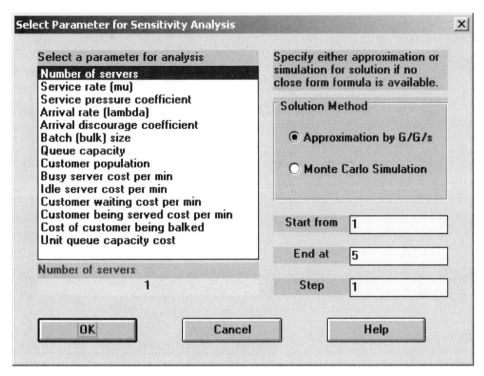

Figure 9.6

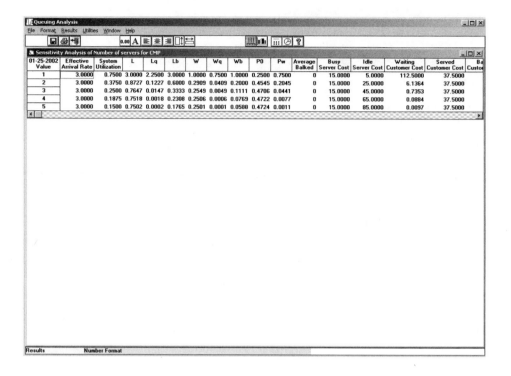

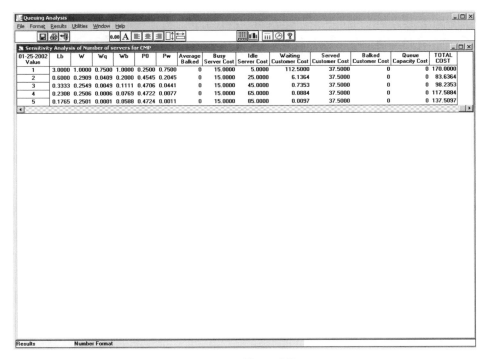

Figure 9.7

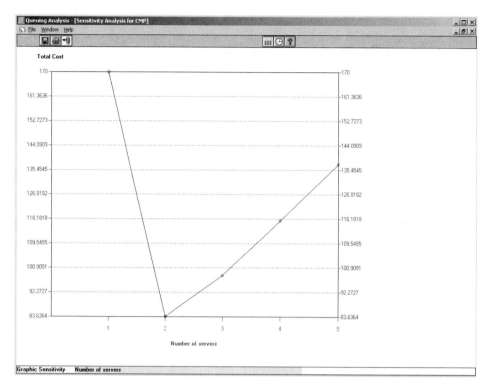

Figure 9.8

CHAPTER **10**

Queuing System Simulation (QSS)

This programming module, Queuing System Simulation (QSS), examines the behavior of a queuing (waiting line) problem. This module can examine a queuing system with customer arrival populations, servers, queues and/or garbage collectors (customer leaving the system without getting service). One can select from 18-probability distributions for arrival and service time patterns. Here one can simulate a queuing system in parallel and/or in series. It also provides nine different selection rules for server operations and 10 for queue disciplines (priority rules).

CMP has a customer order processing system. They have one telephone line with an operator to take an order. They get, on average, three calls per minute (exponentially distributed) and it takes on average 15 seconds to help record the order (exponentially distributed). The number of callers that can be put on hold is unlimited. Potentially CMP has unlimited customers. Once an order is taken, it is passed on to the storekeeper, who then asks the three pickers to collects the items for shipping from the warehouse. The average processing time for each order by the storekeeper is 0.33 minutes (exponentially distributed). Each order picker takes about 0.75 minutes (Normally distributed with a mean of 0.75 minutes and standard deviation of 0.5 minutes) to collect the order for shipping. Figure 10.1 shows the schematic of the CMP order processing system. Here CMP has three queues. After the storekeeper completes the processing of an order, the order is put in the 'out file,' from which each picker will take the order according to first in first out (FIFO) queue discipline rule.

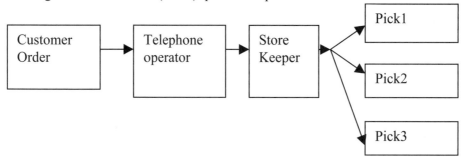

Figure 10.1

In WinQSB, click on **File**, then **New Problem**. You will see an input menu as shown in Figure 10.2. Enter the problem title. In CMP's example, we have nine system components, incoming customer orders (customer), telephone operator (server), storekeeper (server), three order pickers, Pick1, Pick2 and Pick3 (servers) and three queues. The time unit is in minutes. Select **Spreadsheet data** entry format and click **OK.**

The next window you will see is for data input. Here you see a list of edited names in the **Component Name** field. In the **Type** column, enter the appropriate type e.g. Order is C (customer) type; Queue 1,2 and 3 are Q (queue) type; TelOperator, Store and Pick 1, 2, and 3 are S (server) type. Queue capacity is assumed to be infinite for each queue, therefore enter M here. Orders are arriving at the rate of 3 per minute (exponential distribution), therefore, in 'Interarrival Time Distribution' enter 'Exp//0.33.' (right click on this cell and one can see the options available for different distributions). The service time distribution for 'TelOperator' is a negative exponential with a 0.25 minute average time to serve a customer; service time for each 'Pick' is normally distributed with a mean of 0.75 minutes and 0.5 minute standard deviation (NOR/0.75/0.5), (Figure 10.3). Once input is completed, click to **Solve and Analyze** and click again to **Solve Problem**).

You will see a menu for Queuing System Simulation (Figure 10.4). Select any random number seed you want, and enter the length of simulation desired (here it is 4000 minutes). Data collection start time is at minute 300 i.e. the simulation will start collecting data after the first 300 minutes of simulation (here data is to be collected for the steady state only). 'M' for Maximum number of data collections (observations) allows an unlimited number of observations. Now click on 'Simulate.' Once a simulation is completed, the same display will show the current time (in this case approximately 4000 minutes) and the number of observations collected. To see the results click on 'Show Analysis' button.

The screen for Customer Analysis will pop up on the screen (Figure 10.5). To see the performance of the servers, click on Results on the toolbar and select 'show server analysis' (See Figure 10.7). For queue analysis, click on Results on the toolbar and select 'show queue analysis (Figure 10.7).

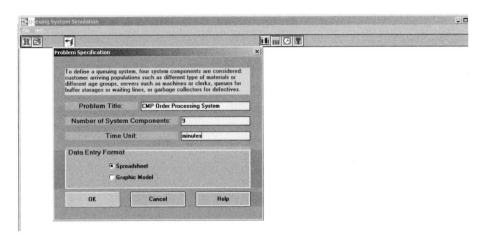

Figure 10.2

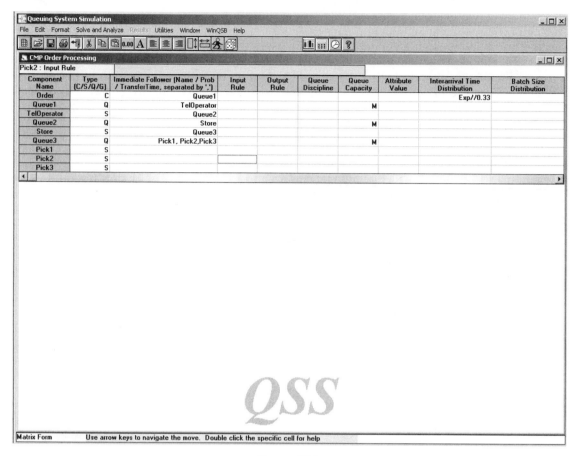

Figure: 10.3

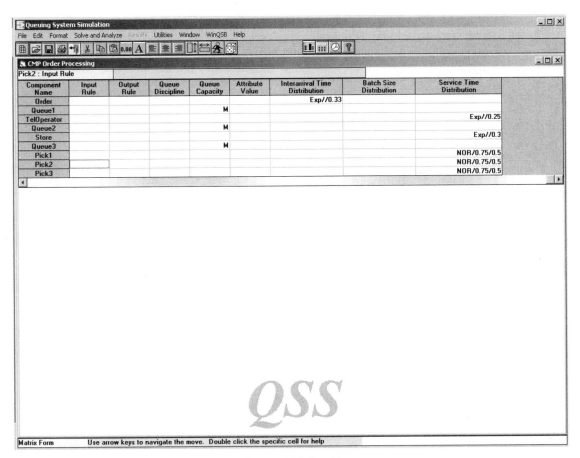

Figure: 10.3 (cont.)

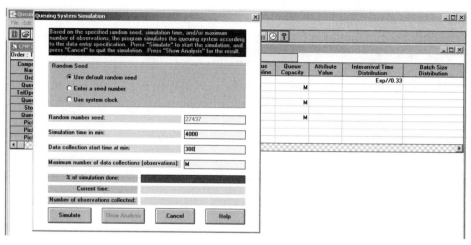

Figure: 10.4

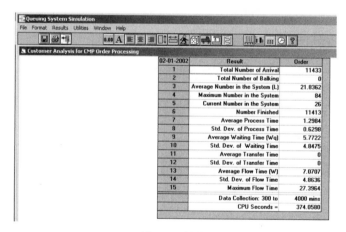

Figure: 10.5

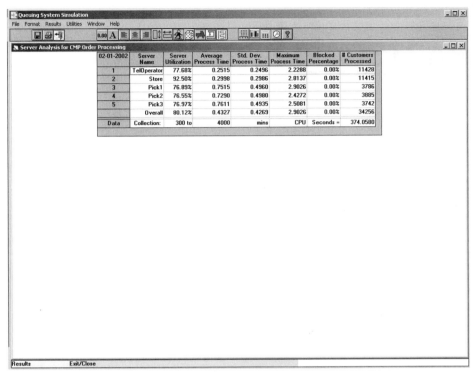

Figure: 10.6

02-01-2002	Queue Name	Average Q. Length (Lq)	Current Q. Length	Maximum Q. Length	Average Waiting (Wq)	Std. Dev. of Wq	Maximum of Wq
1	Queue1	2.5360	5	24	0.8210	0.9339	6.1086
2	Queue2	13.7938	14	76	4.4674	4.5998	23.7624
3	Queue3	1.4991	2	20	0.4859	0.7242	5.4692
	Overall	17.8289	21	76	1.9244	3.2813	23.7624
Data	Collection:	300 to	4000	mins	CPU	Seconds =	374.0580

Figure: 10.7

CHAPTER **11**

Inventory Theory and Systems (ITS)

This programming module, Inventory Theory and Systems (ITS), solves and evaluates inventory control problems. Inventory consists of items in which one has invested capital. It could be materials, parts, semi-finished assembly or finished products. In all inventory issues, one will have to answer two basic questions, how many to buy and when to buy.

This module solves the following types of inventory problems:

EOQ (economic order quantity) problem

EOQ with quantity discount problem

Single period probabilistic (newsboy) problem

Dynamic lot sizing problems using 10 alternative methods

Solving, evaluating, and simulating inventory systems: (s,Q), (s,S), (R,S) and (R,s,S).

Let us look at the basic inventory problem faced by CMP Furniture Company. For the cherry wood used for the making of a chair, the annual requirement is 3600 units. The accounting department has estimated that the cost of preparing an order is $200. The cost of holding a unit of wood is $25 per year. The cost of wood is $100 per unit.

From WinQSB, select **Inventory Theory and System** module. Select **New Problem** and from the next menu select **'Deterministic Demand Economic Order Quantity**

(EOQ) Problem. Enter 'CMP' for the name of the problem, enter 'year' for the time unit, and click OK. (See Figure 11.1)

The next menu is for data input as shown in Figure 11.2. Enter the appropriate values for annual demand, ordering cost, unit holding cost, and the cost of one unit. Here shortages are not allowed, hence the unit shortage cost by default is 'M', a very large value. The supplier is assumed to have large supplies on hand therefore 'Replenishment" is, by default 'M,' a very large value. Now click on **Solve and Analyze**, and select **Solve the Problem**. The next screen will display the solution (Figure 11.3). CMP should order 240 units of cherry wood at a time, at the annual inventory (holding and ordering cost) cost of $6000.00.

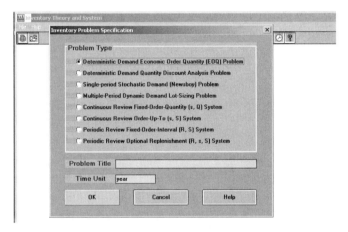

Figure 11.1

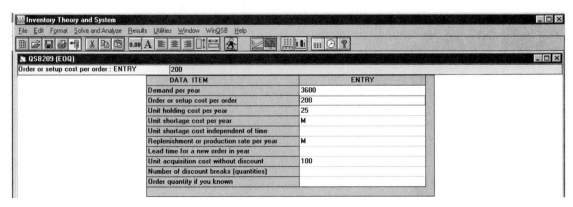

Figure 11.2

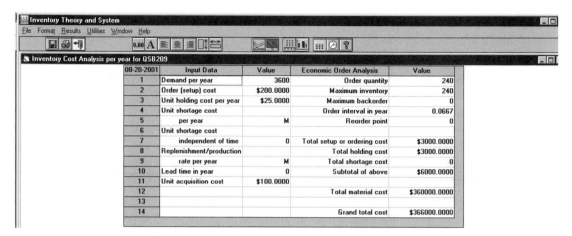

Figure 11.3

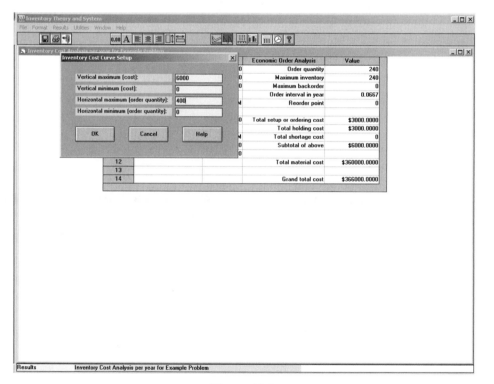

Figure: 11.4

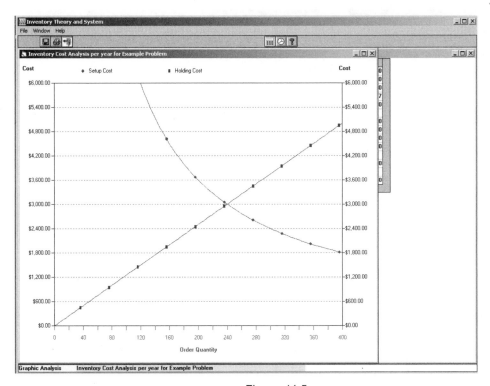

Figure: 11.5

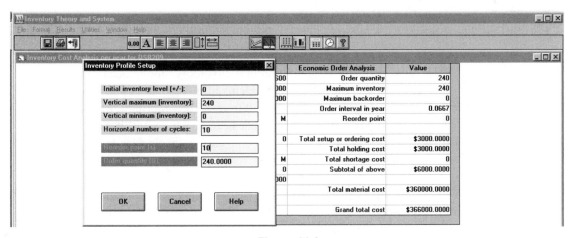

Figure: 11.6

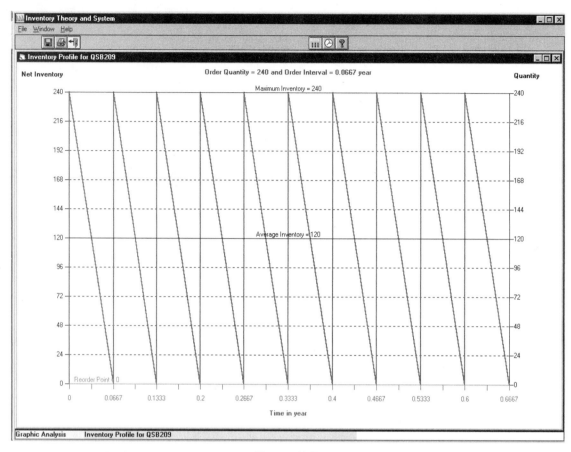

Figure: 11.7

Suppose that CMP wants to investigate another inventory modelbecause not all assumptions of the classical EOQ model are met. Demand is 3600 units per year but it is normally distributed with a standard deviation of 50 units. The ordering cost is $200 per order, the cost of one unit is $100, and holding cost is $25/year. CMP has a stochastic demand, 100% of shortage is back ordered, and the cost of backorder is $20. Let's examine a 'Continuous Review Fixed-Order-Quantity (s, Q) System,' to explore a solution.

Click **New** on WinQSB in 'Inventory Theory and Systems' module. Select **continuous review fixed-order-quantity** (s, Q) system. Enter CMP for problem title, click OK (Figure 11.8). Enter data as shown in Figure 11.9. Here the lead time for receiving wood is a constant of 20 days. (The computation for the Constant value is 20 days/360 days equal to 0.0555).

On the tool bar, click on **Solve and Analyze** and then click **Solve**. Select **Solve the Optimal** (s, Q) and click **Solve** (Figure 11.10). Figure 11.11 displays the solution. Note that the optimal reorder point is 215.9491 units, the optimal order quantity is 245.3235, and the optimal inventory cost is $6540.297. The service level is 91.4818% (100-8.5182) during the lead-time. CMP management thinks that the service level during lead-time should be 98%. On the tool bar click the **Solve and Analyze** button and choose **Solve the Problem** from the menu. Click on **Solve** with desired service level (%) during lead-time option and enter 98 in the corresponding cell. (Figure 11.12) Click OK. Figure 11.13 displays the solution. The reorder point is now 224.0063 and total inventory relevant costs are $6630.892. Figure 11.14 displays the graphic profile for this problem.

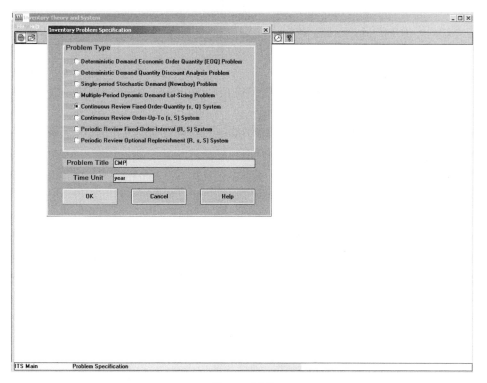

Figure: 11.8

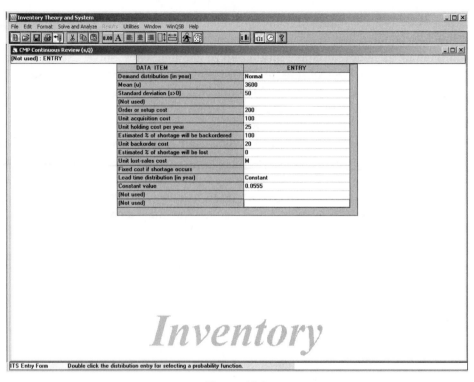

Figure: 11.9

Figure: 11.10

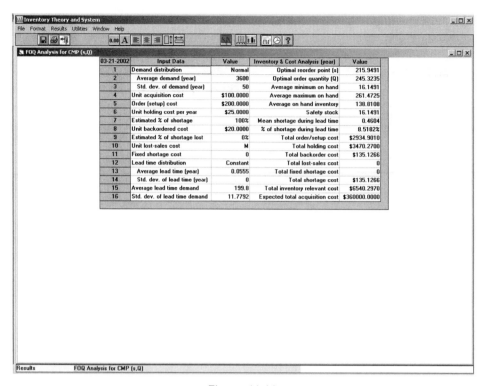

03-21-2002	Input Data	Value	Inventory & Cost Analysis (year)	Value
1	Demand distribution	Normal	Optimal reorder point (s)	215.9491
2	Average demand (year)	3600	Optimal order quantity (Q)	245.3235
3	Std. dev. of demand (year)	50	Average minimum on hand	16.1491
4	Unit acquisition cost	$100.0000	Average maximum on hand	261.4725
5	Order (setup) cost	$200.0000	Average on hand inventory	138.8108
6	Unit holding cost per year	$25.0000	Safety stock	16.1491
7	Estimated % of shortage	100%	Mean shortage during lead time	0.4604
8	Unit backordered cost	$20.0000	% of shortage during lead time	8.5182%
9	Estimated % of shortage lost	0%	Total order/setup cost	$2934.9010
10	Unit lost-sales cost	M	Total holding cost	$3470.2700
11	Fixed shortage cost	0	Total backorder cost	$135.1266
12	Lead time distribution	Constant	Total lost-sales cost	0
13	Average lead time (year)	0.0555	Total fixed shortage cost	0
14	Std. dev. of lead time (year)	0	Total shortage cost	$135.1266
15	Average lead time demand	199.8	Total inventory relevant cost	$6540.2970
16	Std. dev. of lead time demand	11.7792	Expected total acquisition cost	$360000.0000

Figure: 11.11

Figure: 11.12

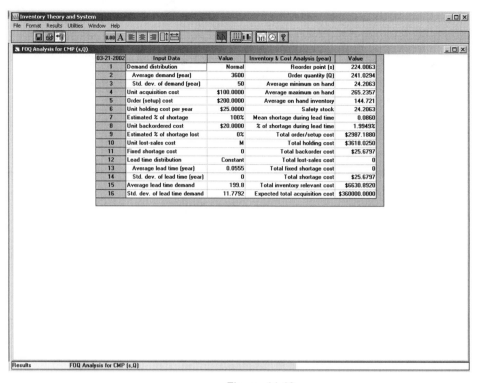

Figure: 11.13

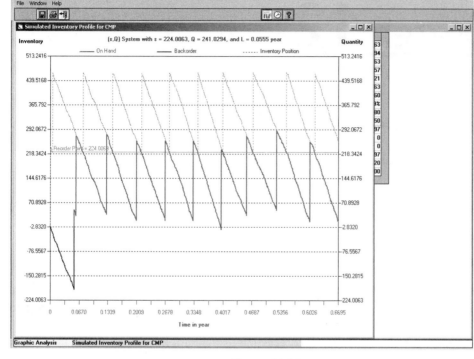

Figure: 11.14

CHAPTER 12

Forecasting (FC)

This programming module, Forecasting (FC), performs time series forecasting, simple linear regression and multiple linear regression. Both time series techniques and regression are used for forecasting.

This module performs time series forecasting using the following methods:

Simple average

Simple moving average

Weighted moving average

Moving average with linear trend

Single exponential smoothing

Single exponential smoothing with linear trend

Double exponential smoothing

Double exponential smoothing with linear trend

Linear regression

Holt-Winters additive algorithm

Holt-Winters multiplicative algorithm

CMP likes to predict demand for their furniture based on family income. A small number of data was collected for preliminary study. From WinQSB select the **Forecasting** (FC) module and click on **New Problem**. The problem type is **Linear Regression**. As shown in Figure 12.1, enter the problem title CMP, for the number of factors (variables), enter two, and CMP has ten observations for the pilot study. Click OK. In the next data input, enter the data as shown in Figure 12.2. Here the column headings are edited using the edit option from the toolbar. The next step is to solve the problem. On the toolbar, click **Solve and Analyze**, and then click perform linear regression. Select Demand as dependent variable, and select all other factors as independent variables (Figure 12.3), and click OK. Figure 12.4 shows the output of regression analysis. The regression equation/model is demand= 91.5821 + 0.0011* Income. The R-square is 96.12%. To display an ANOVA table, click on the result on toolbar and select 'show ANOVA.' The ANOVA result is shown in Figure 12.5. The correlation analysis is obtained by selecting 'show correlation analyses from result on toolbar. The correlation analysis is shown in Figure 12.6.

CMP wants to predict demand for their furniture for a family whose income is $45,000. Click on **Solve & Analyze**, and click on perform estimation and prediction. Next, in the input (Figure 12.7) menu enter 5% as significance level; next click on **'enter value for independent variable'** and you will get the next menu for entering independent variables for which you want to predict the dependent variable, in this case a demand. Enter the values shown in Figure 12.8, and click OK. The prediction result is shown in Figure 12.9. It shows that if the family income is $45,000, the estimated demand will be between 110 and 146.

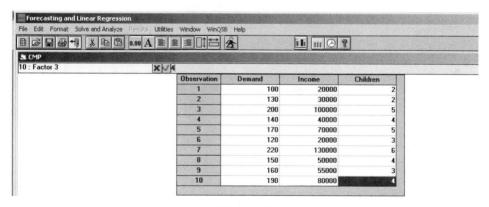

Figure: 12.1

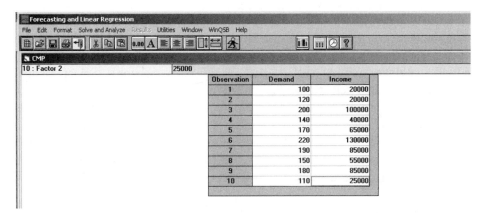

Figure: 12.2

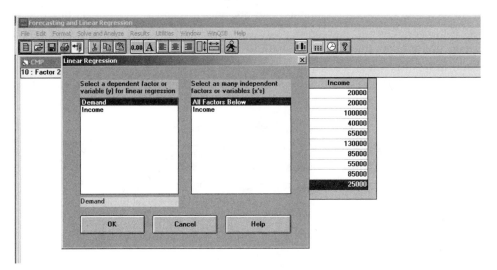

Figure: 12.3

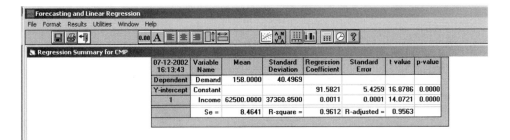

Figure: 12.4

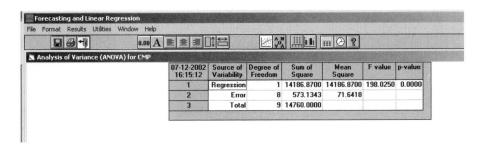

Figure: 12.5

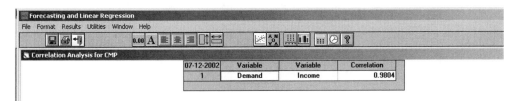

Figure: 12.6

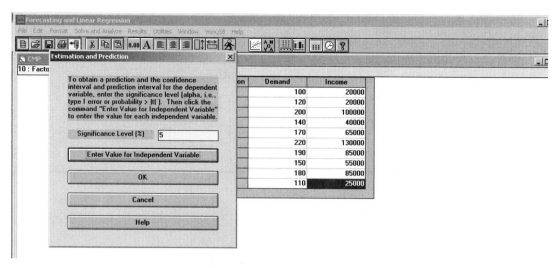

Figure: 12.7

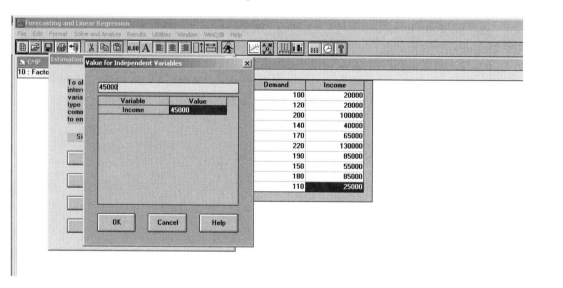

Figure: 12.8

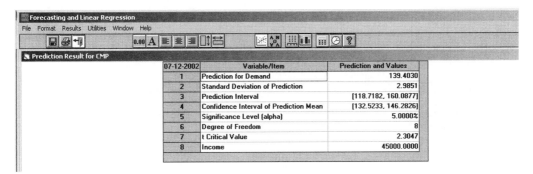

Figure 12.9

CMP is interested in forecasting demand for one of their tables. For the last five weeks, sales figures are 120, 150, 200, 250, and 100. The sales department wants to know how many of this table they can expect to sell next week. Let us examine two simple time series forecasting models, Simple Average and Single Exponential Smoothing technique.

In WinQSB, select 'Forecasting' module. Click on **New Problem**. Select Problem Type: **Time Series Forecasting**. For problem title enter CMP; Time Unit, Week, and for Number of Time Units (Periods), enter 5 (Figure 12.10). Now click OK. In the next data input table enter historical data for past five weeks sales and click **Solve and Analyze**. (Figure 12.11) Now one will see options of twelve forecasting techniques. For simple average (SA) method click on (SA), and enter 1 for number of periods to forecast and click OK (Figure 12.12).   Figure 12.13 shows the results. The forecasted sale for the 6th week is 164 units. The output also shows the four types of error measurements. The graph (Figure 12.14) can be seen by using the command **Show Forecasting in Graph** from the results menu or from the icon on the toolbar.

We can explore another forecasting technique. Click on the **Solve and Analyze** toolbar for the same data. Select 'single exponential smoothing' technique from the forecasting method menu (Figure 12.15).   Now one has to enter the value of the smoothing constant alpha. In this example, the alpha is equal to 0.4. Click OK. Figure 12.16 shows the result. Here the forecast for the 6th week is 157.3120 or 158 units. The graph (Figure 12.17) can be seen by using the command **Show Forecasting in Graph** from the results menu or from the icon on the toolbar.

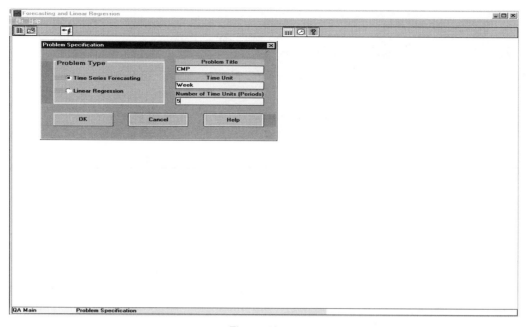

Figure 12.10

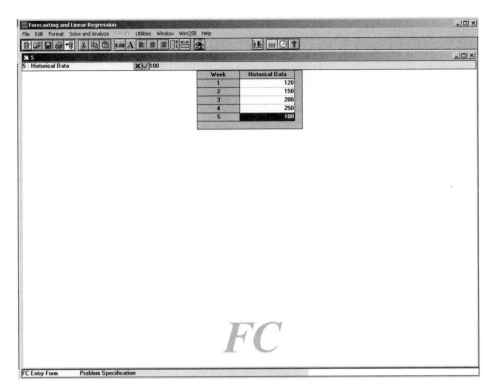

Figure 12.11

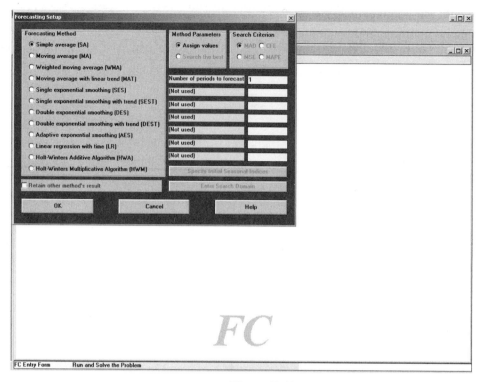

Figure 12.12

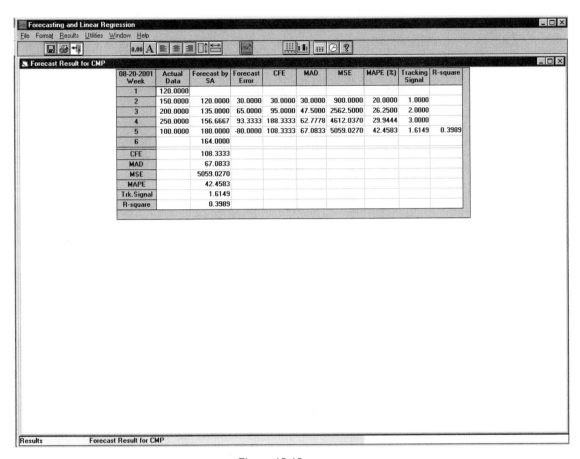

Figure 12.13

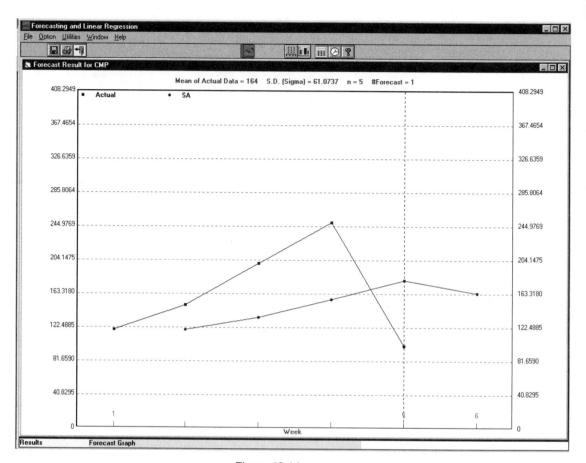

Figure 12.14

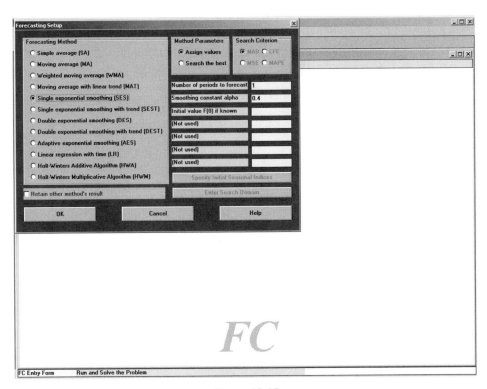

Figure 12.15

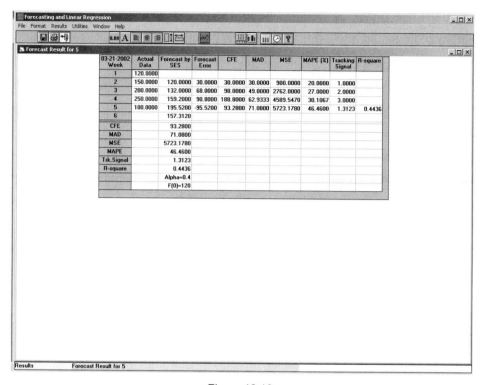

Figure 12.16

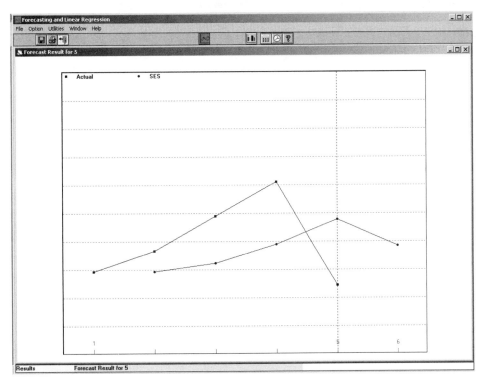

Figure 12.17

Another feature of this Time Series forecasting module is that you can use a number of options for the forecasting technique (Figure: 12.12), and if you select the option of "Retaining other method's results" on the bottom of this menu, it will allow you to view the graphical display of all the results of all the techniques you selected. Here the figure 12.18 shows the actual data, Simple Average (SA) and Single Exponential Smoothing (SES) on the same graph.

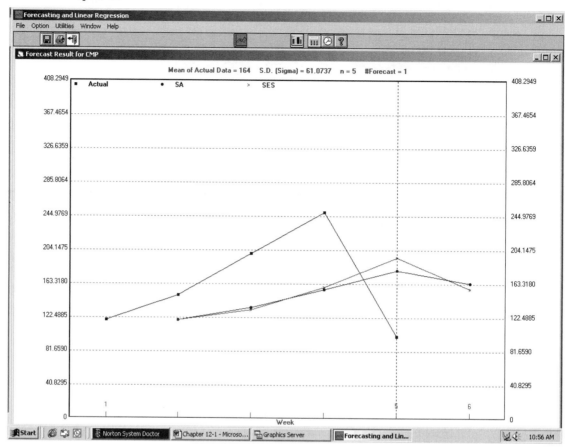

Figure: 12.18

CHAPTER **13**

Decision Analysis (DA)

This programming module, Decision Analysis (DA), solves four types of decision problems: Bayesian analysis, payoff table analysis, decision tree analysis, and zero-sum game theory.

This module has the following features:

- Bayesian analysis: finds posterior probabilities given sample information
- Payoff table: uses seven criteria to make decisions for payoff scenarios
- Decision tree: evaluates expected values for each node and makes a decision
- Two-player zero-sum game: finds the saddle point for the stable solution or optimal probabilities for the unstable solution. Performs game play and Monte Carlo simulation.

CMP wants to develop new furniture to increase their sales. There is a 70% probability that the sales will rise and a 30% probability that the sales will be low. This can be modeled as a decision tree problem. Figure 13.1 shows the situation faced by CMP in decision tree form; the expense of developing the new furniture line and the payoffs of developing the new line based on decision options (develop new furniture or not) and sales scenario.

Open WinQSB, and select the **Decision Analysis** module. Click on **File** and select **New Problem**. In the problem specification select, Decision Tree Analysis, for the **Problem Type**, and enter the information as shown in Figure 13.2, then click **OK**. Here the Node/Events descriptions are edited. Figure 13.3 shows CMP's data entry. Once you've entered the data, click on **Solve and Analyze** and select **Solve the Problem**. Figure 13.4 shows the summarized analysis. After solving the problem, to see the decision tree graph, click on **Show Decision Tree Graph** from the **Results** menu. The setup menu will appear. Select items as displayed in Figure 13.5. The decision tree with expected values is shown in Figure 13.6.

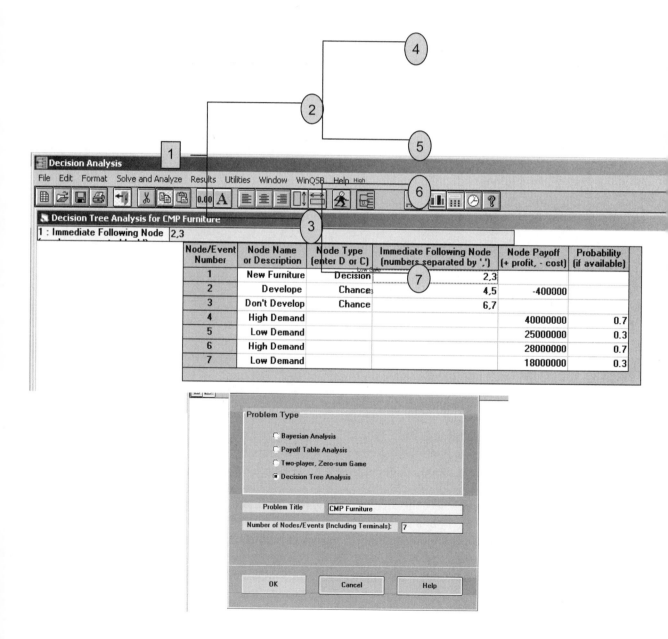

Figure 13.3

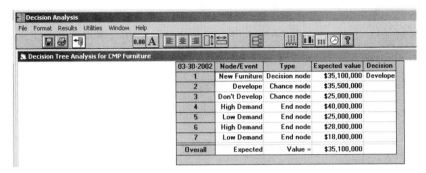

Figure 13.4

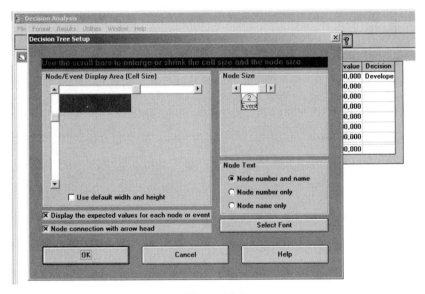

Figure 13.5

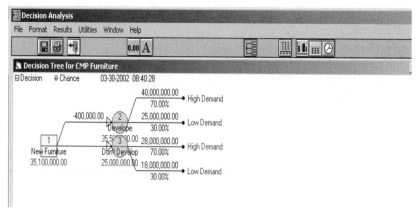

Figure 13.6

CHAPTER **14**

Markov Process (MKPA)

This programming module, Markov Process (MKPA), solves and analyzes the Markov process. This program has the following capabilities:

- Solve steady state probabilities
- Perform step-by-step Markov process
- Perform time dependent performance analysis
- Analyze the total cost or return

CMP's marketing department has analyzed the data regarding brand loyalty to CMP products. The transition matrix is shown below in Figure 14.1. CMP management wants to examine the brand switching behavior of it customers.

At present	Next purchase		
	CMP	A	B
CMP	0.8	0.15	0.05
A	0.2	0.65	0.15
B	0.3	0.1	0.6

Figure 14.1

To explore this problem, open WinQSB, and select the **Markov Process** module. Click on **File**, select **New Problem**, and enter the information as shown in Figure 14.2. Click **OK**. The next screen is for the input data. Enter the transition probabilities and cost data

as shown in Figure 14.3. To solve this problem, use the command **Solve Steady State** from **Solve and Analyze** on the toolbar. The steady state solution is shown in Figure 14.4. Selecting the command **Markov Process Step** from **Solve and Analyze** will display the screen as seen in Figure 14.5. In that screen, enter 1 in the cell for the **Initial State Probability** of CMP and 2 for **the number of time periods from initial** and click **Next Period**. The resulting state probability will be displayed.

Parametric analysis on the nature of time dependency can be performed by selecting **Time Parametric Analysis** from the **Solve and Analyze** menu. CMP wants to know how the expected cost will change over time after the CMP product is bought. Figure 14.6 shows the specification of parametric analysis and Figure 14.7 shows the result of the analysis in tabular form and Figure 14.8 displays it in the graphical form.

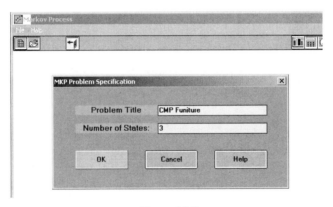

Figure 14.2

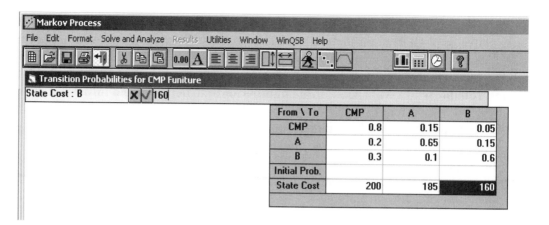

Figure 14.3

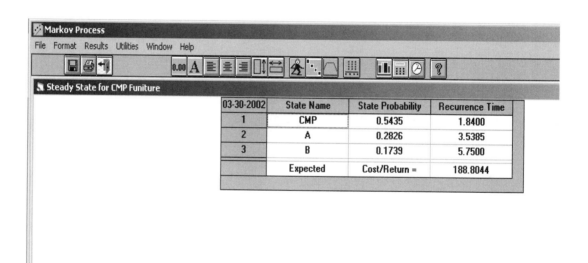

Figure 14.4

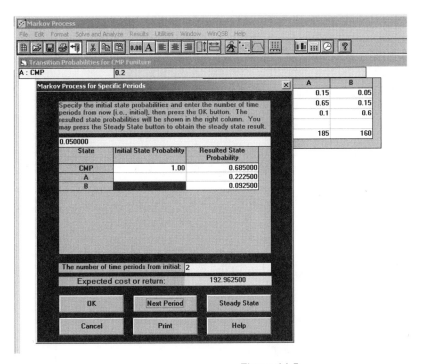

Figure 14.5

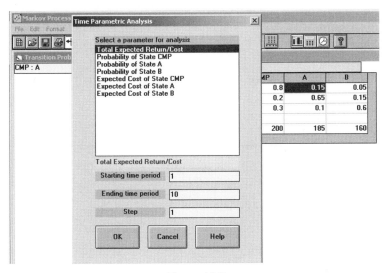

Figure 14.6

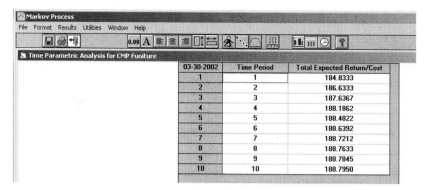

Figure 14.7

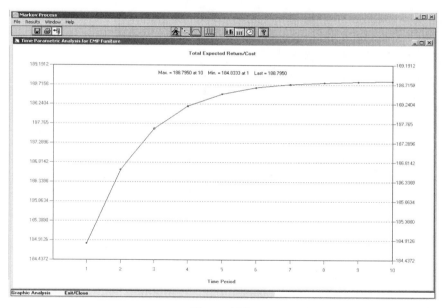

Figure 14.8

CHAPTER **15**

Quality Control Charts (QCC)

This programming module, Quality Control Charts (QCC), constructs quality control charts and performs graphical analyses. A quality control chart is a graphical display of the result of quality characteristics measured over time or samples. Quality characteristics either are expressed in numerical values (variable data) or in terms of a number of nonconformities (attribute data). This module provides a variety of control charts for both types of data.

The QCC module can construct 21 different control charts for variable data: such as X-bar; R-bar; Standard Deviation (SD); variance; individuals; median; midrange; cusum for (a) mean, (b) range, and (c) SD; trend for mean and individuals; geometric moving average for mean and individuals; moving average for mean and individuals; modified control of mean, individuals; acceptance control for both mean and individuals.

This module can also construct 15 different control charts for attribute data: such as p-chart (proportion non-conforming); np-chart (number non- conforming); C-chart number of defects); u-chart (average number of defects); U-chart (demerits per unit); cusum for p (proportion non-conforming); C (number of defects); geometric moving average for p, C; moving average for p, C; standardized p, np, C and u.

CMP's quality department wants to know if one of their processes is working properly or not. The process cuts a piece of wood ten inches long. The tolerance is ± 0.1." Data was collected and is shown in Figure 15.2. Let us examine some of the basic charts for this process.

In WinQSB, select the **Quality Control Chart** module. Click on **File** and select **New Problem**. Now in the QCC problem specification form, click on variable data and subgroup vertically (data are in column form). The **Problem Title** is CMP. The **Number of Quality Characteristics** is 1. The **Size of Subgroups** is 5. The **Number of Subgroups** is 10 (there are in total 50 data points), now click **OK** (Figure 15.1). The next screen is the data entry form. The CMP data is entered as shown in Figure 15.2. Now on the toolbar, click **View**. On the pop up menu, select **USL/LSL** to enter the process specification limits (Figure 15.3). In the CMP case the USL is 10.1 and LSL is 9.9 (Figure 15.4). Now from **View** on the toolbar, click on **Data Entry** to go back to the data. Next select **Setup** under **Gallery** on the toolbar. Figure 15.5 shows the setup options. The example shows the setup for R-bar chart, UCL/LCL set as 3 and -3 σ and the rest of the selections are the default settings. Click **OK** and the R-bar chart (Figure 15.6) will appear. To see the X-bar chart for this example, select the **X-bar chart** from the **Gallery** menu and one will see the X-bar chart (Figure 15.7).

CMP also wants to monitor their process capability. For that, use the command **Process Capability Analysis** from **Analysis** on the toolbar to display the process capability analysis based on USL/LSL value entered before. Figure 15.8 shows the process capability.

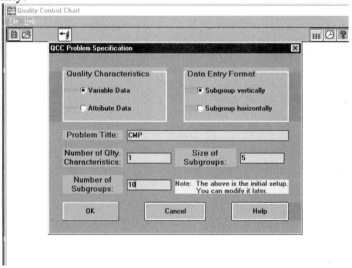

Figure 15.1

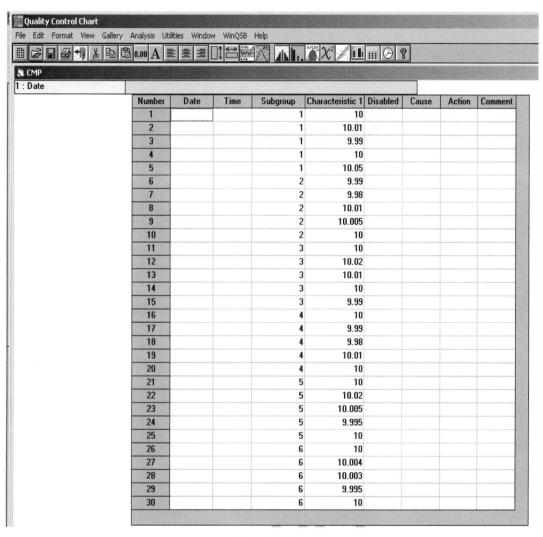

Figure 15.2

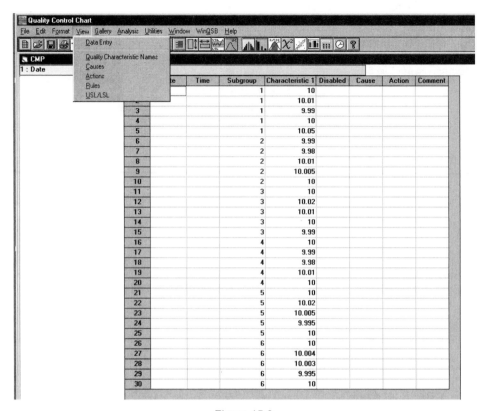

Figure 15.3

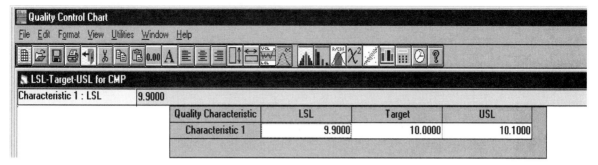

Figure 15.4

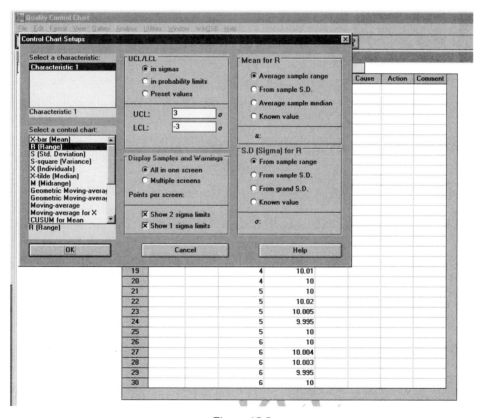

Figure 15.5

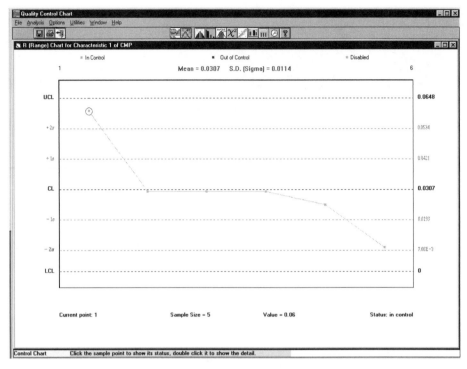

Figure 15.6

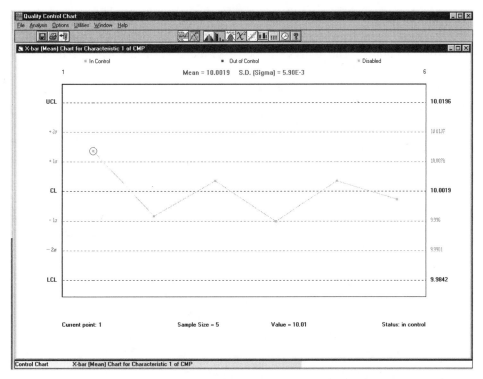

Figure 15.7

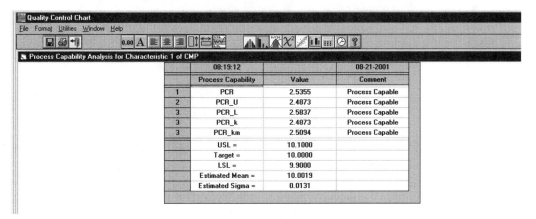

Figure 15.8

CMP takes a sample of 4 parts of chair legs every hour and looks for surface blemishes. If there are more than two blemishes on the leg, the leg does not conform. Data is collected over 10 hours. The analysis to be performed over is a C-chart, part of attribute analysis.

In WinQSB, select **Quality Control Chart**, and click on **File** and select **New Problem**. Figure 15.9 shows the complete specifications for this problem. Click **OK**, and spreadsheet data entry form is displayed. Enter data as shown in Figure 15.10. Once the data entry is complete, click on **Gallery** and select **Setup**. Enter data as shown in Figure 15.11. Now click again on **Gallery** and select **C (Number of nonconforming) Chart**. Figure 15.12 shows the C-bar chart.

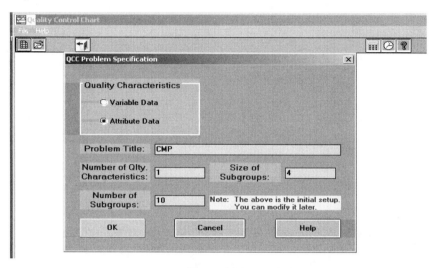

Figure 15.9

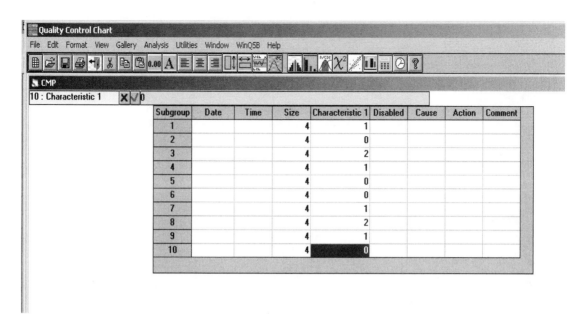

Figure 15.10

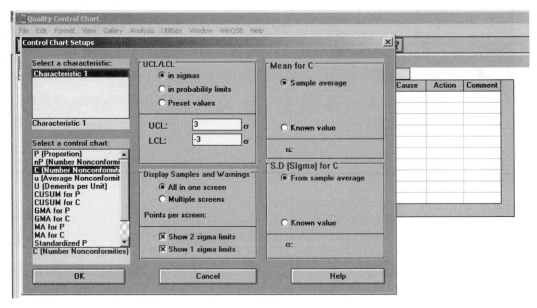

Figure 15.11

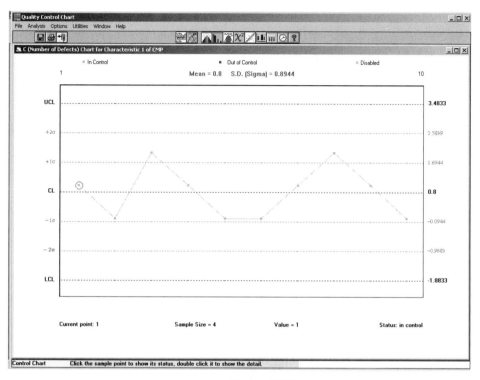

Figure 15.12

CHAPTER **16**

Acceptance Sampling Analysis (ASA)

This programming module, Acceptance Sampling Analysis (ASA), develops and analyzes acceptance sampling plans for variable and attribute quality characteristics. Acceptance sampling deals with whether a production lot or process is acceptable. One selects a random sample or samples, from the lot produced and checks for defects. If this inspection shows more defects than acceptable, then the lot can be rejected (single sampling plan) or could be subjected to a second sampling (double sampling plan). Also, if the combined number of defects exceed the acceptable level, one may reject the lot and subject the lot for 100 percent inspection if desirable.

This module has the following capabilities:

Acceptance sampling analysis for attributes:
    Single Sampling
    Double Sampling
    Multiple Sampling
    Sequential Sampling
    Chain Sampling
    Continuous Sampling
    Skip-lot Sampling

Acceptance sampling analysis for variables:
    Single Sampling- Sample Mean
    Single Sampling: Controlling Fraction Nonconforming – k Method
    Single Sampling: Controlling Fraction Nonconforming – M Method
    Sequential Sampling

Construct OC, AOQ, ATI, ASN, and Cost curves

Compute producer's risk (α) and consumer's risk (β)

Search sampling plan using weighted α/β or AOQL

Determine acceptable and rejectable quality levels.

Perform what-if-analysis

Perform sequential sampling process

Provide description for sampling plan operation

Allow to specify probability function for attribute data

CMP wants to develop a sampling plan for their furniture manufacturing. Once a batch of furniture is made, a quality check for appearance is made. Normally they produce their furniture in lots of 50. The manager of quality wants to develop a single sampling plan.

In WinQSB, select the **Acceptance Sampling Analysis** module. Click on **File** and select **New Problem** from the menu. Select **Acceptance Sampling for: Attributes** and for **Type of Sampling Plan**, select Single Sampling and click **OK** (Figure 16.1). Figure 16.2 shows the spreadsheet input form. Enter the data as shown. Now click on **Solve and Analyze** and select the **Draw OC Curve** option. The next data spreadsheet will ask for any additional plans i.e. sample size and number of defectives acceptable. We will keep the original plan, lot size of 50 and two defective parts (Figure 16.3). Now click **OK**. The OC curve is displayed in Figure 16.4. Again click on **Solve and Analyze** and select the **Analyze Current Plan** option. Part of the answer is shown in Figure 16.5. Now click on **Results** on the toolbar and select **Show Current Plan Description** and the plan is explained as shown in Figure 16.6. The last thing CMP wants to determine is the producer and consumer's risk. Click on **Solve and Analyze** on the toolbar, and select **Determine Producer's/Consumer's Risks** option. The result is shown in Figure 16.7.

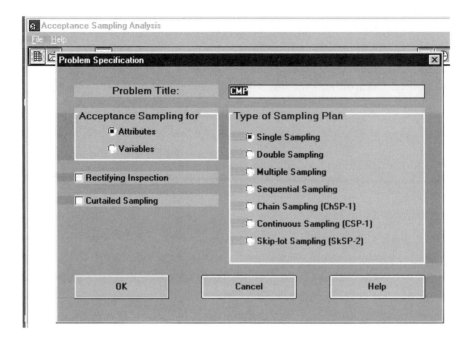

Figure 16.1

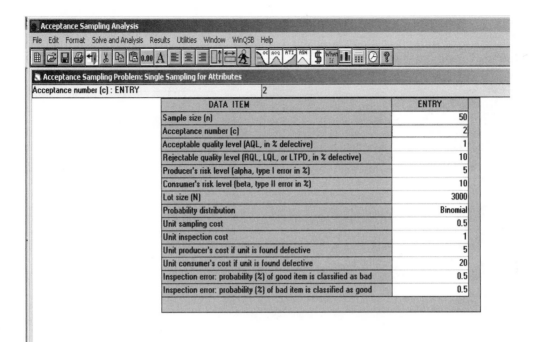

Figure 16.2

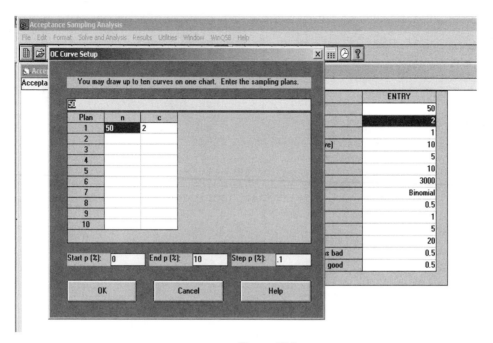

Figure 16.3

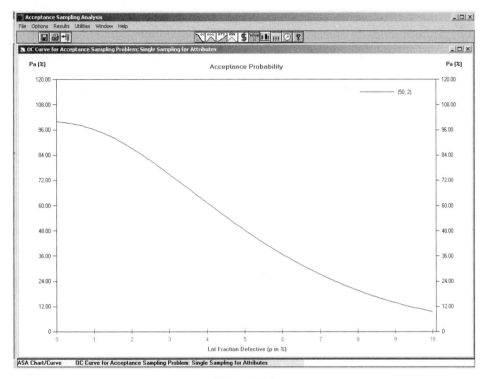

Figure 16.4

Acceptance Sampling Analysis — File Format Results Utilities Window Help

Analysis for Acceptance Sampling Problem: Single Sampling for Attributes

No.	P (%)	Pe (%)	Pa (%)	AOQ (%)	ASN	ATI	Total Cost
0	0	0.5000	99.7945	0	50	56.0631	$82.46
1	1.0000	1.4900	96.1400	0.9464	50	163.8710	$768.47
2	2.0000	2.4800	87.2851	1.7241	50	425.0899	$1,533.62
3	3.0000	3.4700	74.9243	2.2346	50	789.7331	$2,280.28
4	4.0000	4.4600	61.3304	2.4639	50	1190.753	$2,933.45
5	5.0000	5.4500	48.2573	2.4561	50	1576.409	$3,462.45
6	6.0000	6.4400	36.7324	2.2802	50	1916.394	$3,870.30
7	7.0000	7.4300	27.1812	2.0058	50	2198.154	$4,177.74
8	8.0000	8.4200	19.6270	1.6912	50	2421.003	$4,411.01
9	9.0000	9.4100	13.8698	1.3784	50	2590.841	$4,594.64
10	10.0000	10.4000	9.6138	1.0936	50	2716.392	$4,748.30
11	11.0000	11.3900	6.5479	0.8503	50	2806.836	$4,886.17
12	12.0000	12.3800	4.3884	0.6525	50	2870.541	$5,017.55
13	13.0000	13.3700	2.8973	0.4982	50	2914.529	$5,148.01
14	14.0000	14.3600	1.8861	0.3822	50	2944.360	$5,280.42
15	15.0000	15.3500	1.2115	0.2980	50	2964.260	$5,416.01
16	16.0000	16.3400	0.7683	0.2390	50	2977.335	$5,554.98
17	17.0000	17.3300	0.4813	0.1995	50	2985.802	$5,697.03
18	18.0000	18.3200	0.2979	0.1743	50	2991.212	$5,841.64
19	19.0000	19.3100	0.1823	0.1597	50	2994.623	$5,988.26
20	20.0000	20.3000	0.1102	0.1525	50	2996.748	$6,136.39
21	21.0000	21.2900	0.0659	0.1506	50	2998.055	$6,285.61
22	22.0000	22.2800	0.0390	0.1523	50	2998.849	$6,435.60
23	23.0000	23.2700	0.0228	0.1566	50	2999.327	$6,586.12
24	24.0000	24.2600	0.0132	0.1625	50	2999.611	$6,737.00
25	25.0000	25.2500	0.0076	0.1697	50	2999.777	$6,888.10
26	26.0000	26.2400	0.0043	0.1777	50	2999.874	$7,039.36
27	27.0000	27.2300	0.0024	0.1864	50	2999.929	$7,190.71
28	28.0000	28.2200	0.0013	0.1955	50	2999.961	$7,342.12
29	29.0000	29.2100	0.0007	0.2051	50	2999.979	$7,493.57
30	30.0000	30.2000	0.0004	0.2151	50	2999.989	$7,645.04
31	31.0000	31.1900	0.0002	0.2254	50	2999.994	$7,796.52
32	32.0000	32.1800	0.0001	0.2360	50	2999.997	$7,948.01
33	33.0000	33.1700	0.0001	0.2469	50	2999.998	$8,099.51
34	34.0000	34.1600	0.0000	0.2582	50	2999.999	$8,251.00

Result/Analysis   Analysis for Acceptance Sampling Problem: Single Sampling for Attributes

Figure 16.5

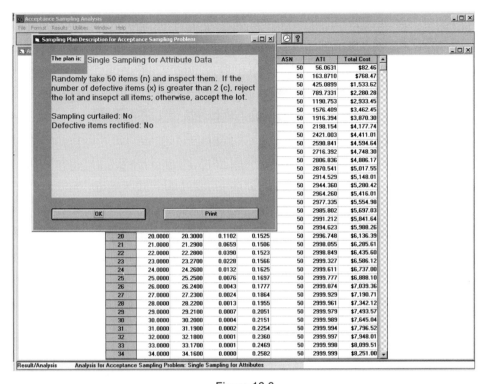

Figure 16.6

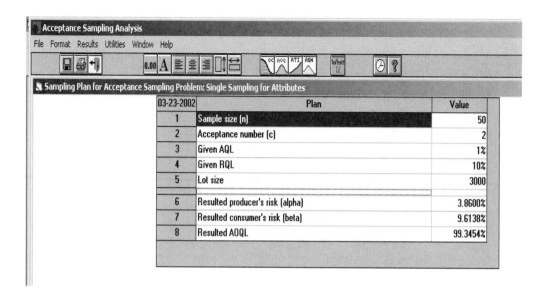

Figure 16.7

CHAPTER 17

Job Scheduling (JOB)

This programming module, Job Scheduling (JOB), solves job shop and flow shop scheduling problems. The module gives options of various heuristics to solve scheduling problems.

The Job Scheduling program has fifteen dispatching rules for job shop problems and seven rules for flow shop problems, including complete enumeration of permutation schedules.

FLOW SHOP

In a flow shop, there are n jobs waiting to be processed on m machines. All jobs have the same routing. A feasible solution consists of jobs that are scheduled on each machine without violating the machine's capacities.

CMP has a small shop with four machines. There are at present four jobs to be scheduled. Data is as shown in Figure 17.2. In WinQSB, select the **Job Scheduling** option and click on **File** and select **New Problem**. Enter CMP as the **Title** and enter four as the **Number of Jobs to be Scheduled,** the **Number of Machines or Workers,** and the **Maximum Number of Operations per Job**. Then check **All jobs have same machine/worker sequence** and click **OK** (Figure 17.1). The next screen is for the data input. Input the appropriate data (do not forget to scroll to right for more data input). (Figure 17.2 and 17.3) The next step is to solve this problem. Click on **Solve and**

Analyze.   Here we have selected Gupta's Method for the **Solution Method**, and the **Objective Criterion** is Cmax (min. makespan) as shown in Figure 17.4.   Click **OK** and the computer will display the solution (Figure 17.5).   Now to display the machine schedule, go to **Results** on the toolbar and select **Show Machine Schedule**, and it will be displayed (Figure 17.6).   To display the Gantt chart for the machine schedule, click on **Results** on the toolbar, select **Show Gantt chart for Machine**, and the computer screen will display (Figure 17.7).   To display a Gantt chart for the job schedule, click on **Results** on the toolbar and select **Show Gantt chart for Job,** and the chart will be displayed on the screen (Figure 17.8).   To see the summary of job sequence, click on **Results** on the toolbar, select **Show Job Sequence,** and the screen will display the job sequence (Figure 17.9).   There are a number of performance measures available for the shop.   Suppose CMP wants to know the machine utilization for this problem, click on **Results** on the toolbar, and select **Show Performance Analysis**.   One will see the option menu as shown in Figure 17.10. Click on Machine Utilization for the **Category** and column chart 2D for the **Display Type;** then click **OK**.   The screen will display the column chart for the machine utilization (Figure 17.11).

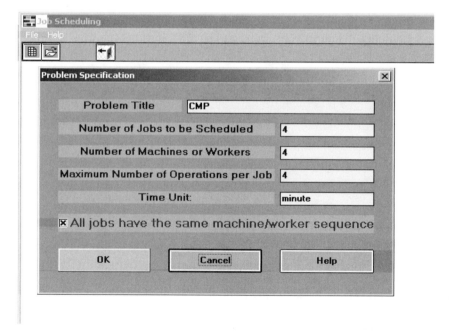

Figure 17.1

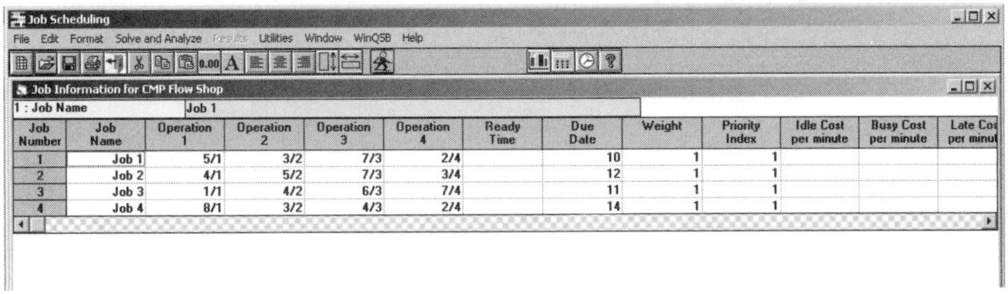

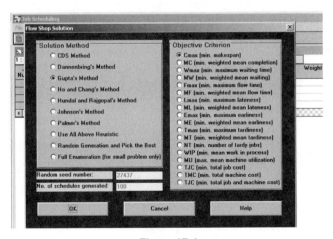

Figure 17.2

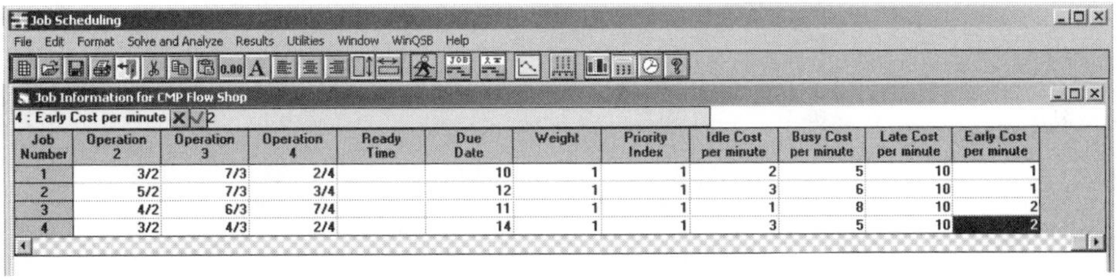

Figure 17.3

Figure 17.4

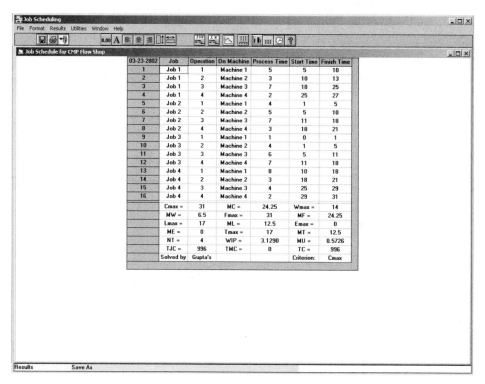

Figure 17.5

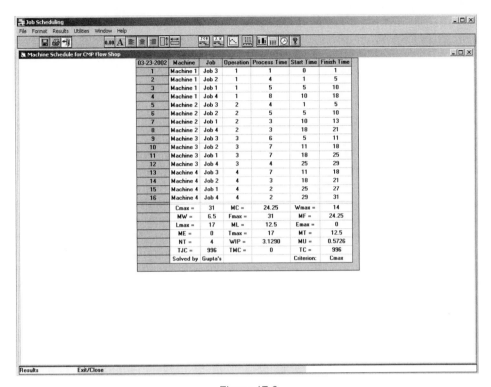

Figure 17.6

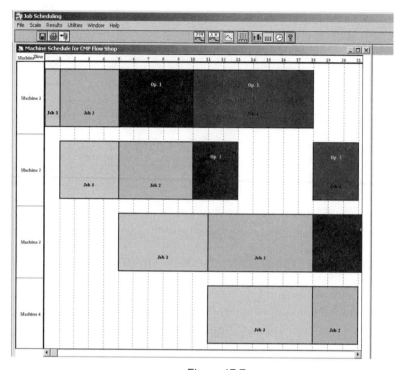

Figure 17.7

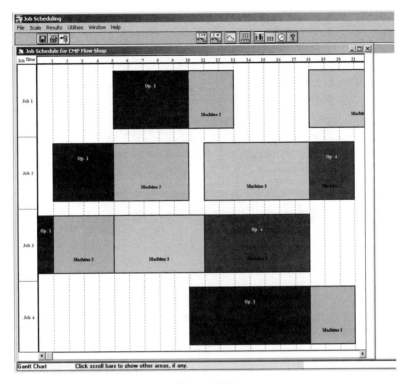

Figure 17.8

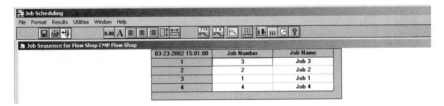

Figure 17.9

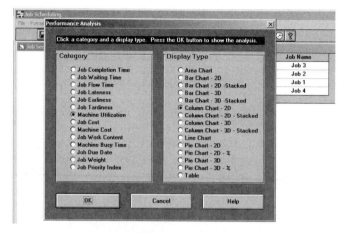

Figure 17.10

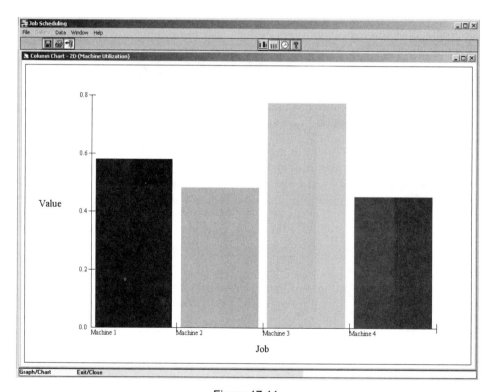

Figure 17.11

JOB SHOP

In a job shop, there are n jobs to be processed on m machines. Each job has its own routing/sequence for processing. A feasible solution here is defined as assigning the job operations to machines without violating the routing and machine capacity.

Suppose CMP has four jobs to be processed on four machines. Data for this problem is shown in Figure 17.13. In WinQSB click on **Job Scheduling,** and then click on **File** and select **New Problem**. Enter the data as shown in Figure 17.12, (make sure you do not check the box that says: **All jobs have the same machine/worker sequence**) and click **OK**. The next screen is for the job data; enter the values as shown in Figure 17.13. Now select **Solve and Analyze** on the toolbar and you will see the options for the **Solution Method** and **Objective Criterion** (Figure 17.14). For our problem select SPT for **Primary Heuristic,** and for **Tiebreaker**, choose random. Now click **OK**. Figure 17.15 displays the solution for the job schedule. To see a Gantt chart for the job, click on **Results** on the toolbar, select **Show Gantt Chart for Job,** and the Gantt chart will be displayed as in Figure 17.16. To display the machine schedule, click on **Results** on the toolbar and select **Show Machine Schedule** and the output will be displayed as shown in Figure 17.17. The Gantt chart for the machine schedule can be seen by clicking on **Results** on the toolbar and selecting **Show Gantt Chart for Machine**; it will be displayed as shown in Figure 17.18. As in a flow shop, there a are number of performance measurements available for a job shop. Click on **Results** on the toolbar, select **Show Performance**, and you will see the option menu (Figure 17.19). Here we select again machine utilization and column chart-2D, and then click **OK**. Figure 17.20 displays the column chart for machine utilization.

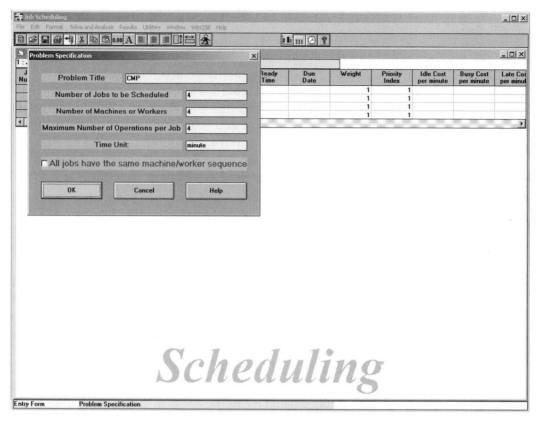

Figure 17.12

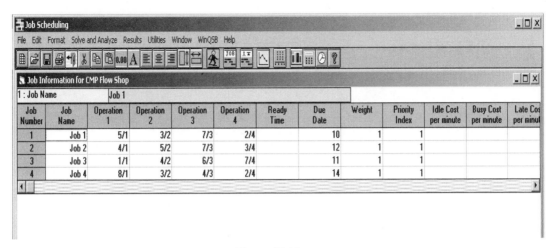

Figure 17.13

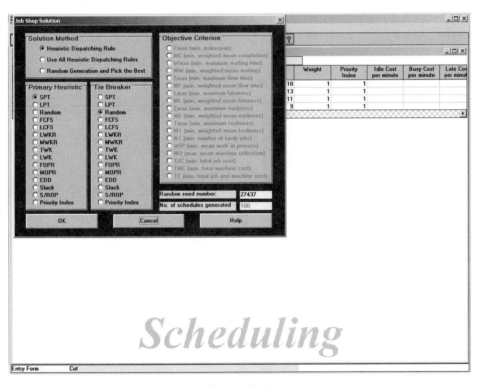

Figure 17.14

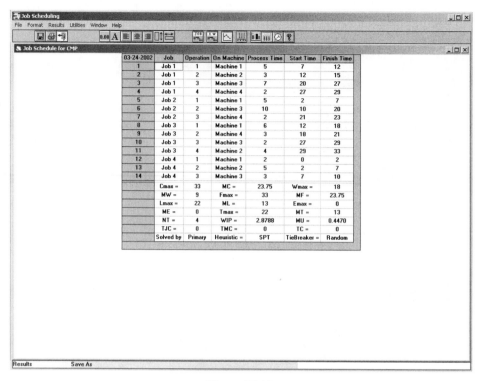

Figure 17.15

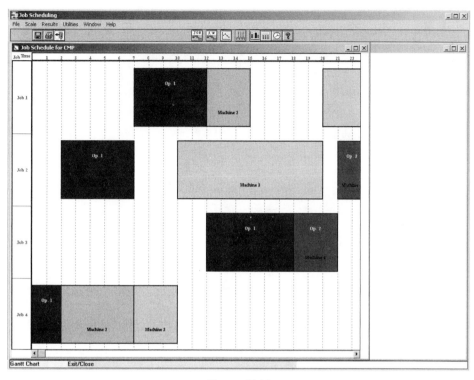

Figure 17.16

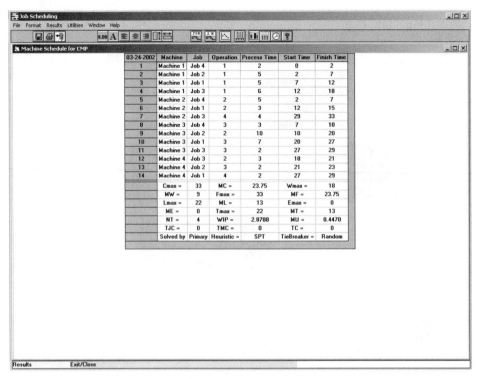

Figure 17.17

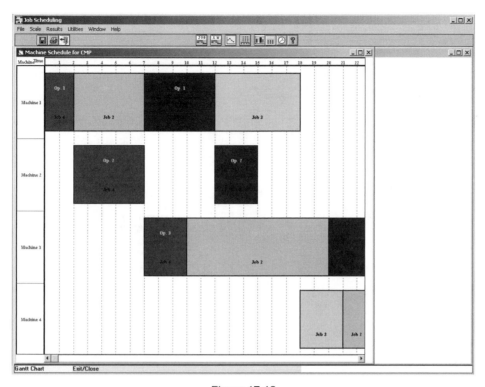

Figure 17.18

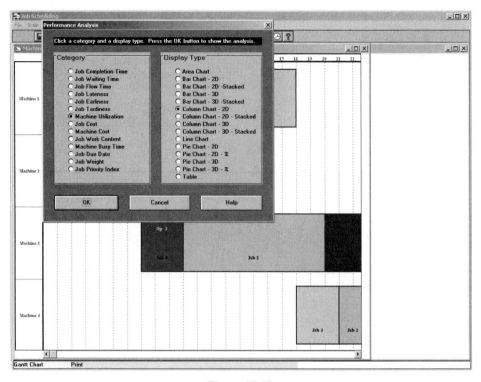

Figure 17.19

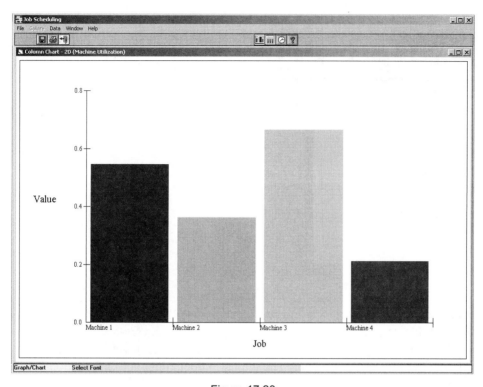

Figure 17.20

CHAPTER **18**

Aggregate Planning (AP)

This programming module, Aggregate Planning (AP), solves aggregate production planning problems (AP). Aggregate planning generally covers a planning period of a year or less, addressing the issue of broad labor requirements, inventory, and the capacity for meeting the forecasted demand. The typical output consists of production schedules, labor requirements, inventory levels, labor overtime, and subcontracting outputs. This module gives three options for solving aggregate planning: simple model, transportation model, and general linear programming model. The simple model allows one to use 10 different strategies for the AP problem, whereas transportation and general LP models give the optimal solution.

The CMP production manager is preparing four quarters of aggregate planning for the next year's high-end chair. The forecasted demands for the next four quarters are 200, 300, 150, and 200, respectively. The rest of the data in terms of capacity, manpower, and costs are shown in Figure 18.1.

To solve this problem, in WinQSB, select the **Aggregate Planning** module, click on **File,** and select **New Problem**. The problem specification menu will be displayed (Figure 18.2). Here CMP is using a general LP model as the **Problem Type,** and all other appropriate categories are checked. The **Number of Planning Periods** is four. Click **OK,** and the data entry spreadsheet will appear (Figure 18.3). Enter all the data and click **Solve and Analyze**, and then select **Solve the Problem**. Figure 18.4 and Figure 18.5 display the solution. To examine the cost analysis, click **Results** on the toolbar and select **Show Cost Analysis** (Figure 18.6). This module also gives the option for graphic solutions for quantity and cost items, displayed in various graphical forms. To select a graphical solution, click on **Results** on the toolbar, and select **Show Graphic Analysis**. The menu will be displayed as shown in Figure 18.7. CMP wants to see graphic solutions for the full time regular time production in a column chart. Select those items in the menu and click **OK**. The module will display the graphic solution (Figure 18.8).

DATA ITEM	Period 1	Period 2	Period 3	Period 4
Forecast Demand	200	300	150	200
Full Time - Initial Number of Employee	4	4	4	4
Full Time - Regular Time Capacity in Hour per Employee	5	5	5	5
Full Time - Regular Time Cost per Hour	10	10	10	10
Full Time - Undertime Cost per Hour	10	10	10	10
Full Time - Overtime Capacity in Hour per Employee	5	5	5	5
Full Time - Overtime Cost per Hour	15	15	15	15
Full Time - Hiring Cost per Employee	50	50	50	50
Full Time - Dismissal Cost per Employee	100	100	100	100
Full Time - Maximum Number of Employee Allowed	20	20	20	20
Full Time - Minimum Number of Employee Allowed	4	4	4	4
Part Time - Initial Number of Employee	0	0	0	0
Part Time - Regular Time Capacity in Hour per Employee	3	3	3	3
Part Time - Regular Time Cost per Hour	12	12	12	12
Part Time - Undertime Cost per Hour	5	5	5	5
Part Time - Overtime Capacity in Hour per Employee	3	3	3	3
Part Time - Overtime Cost per Hour	18	18	18	18
Part Time - Hiring Cost per Employee	20	20	20	20
Part Time - Dismissal Cost per Employee	50	50	50	50
Part Time - Maximum Number of Employee Allowed	5	5	5	5
Part Time - Minimum Number of Employee Allowed	0	0	0	0
Initial Inventory (+) or Backorder (-)	10			
Maximum Ending Inventory Allowed	M	M	M	M
Minimum Ending Inventory (Safety Stock)	10	10	10	10
Unit Inventory Holding Cost	15	15	15	15
Maximum Subcontracting Allowed	M	M	M	M
Unit Subcontracting Cost	50	50	50	50
Maximum Backorder Allowed	M	M	M	M
Unit Backorder Cost	20	20	20	20
Maximum Lost-Sales Allowed	M	M	M	M
Unit Lost-Sales Cost	30	30	30	30
Other Unit Production Cost				
Capacity Requirement in Hour per Unit	1	1	1	1

Figure 18.1

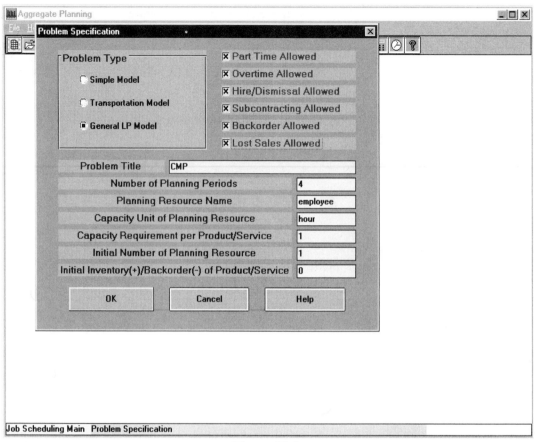

Figure 18.2

Aggregate Planning

File Edit Format Solve and Analyze Results Utilities Window WinQSB Help

Planning Information for CMP (LP Model)

Forecast Demand : Period 1   200

DATA ITEM	Period 1	Period 2	Period 3	Period 4
Forecast Demand	200	300	150	200
Full Time - Initial Number of Employee	4	4	4	4
Full Time - Regular Time Capacity in Hour per Employee	5	5	5	5
Full Time - Regular Time Cost per Hour	10	10	10	10
Full Time - Undertime Cost per Hour	10	10	10	10
Full Time - Overtime Capacity in Hour per Employee	5	5	5	5
Full Time - Overtime Cost per Hour	15	15	15	15
Full Time - Hiring Cost per Employee	50	50	50	50
Full Time - Dismissal Cost per Employee	100	100	100	100
Full Time - Maximum Number of Employee Allowed	20	20	20	20
Full Time - Minimum Number of Employee Allowed	4	4	4	4
Part Time - Initial Number of Employee	0	0	0	0
Part Time - Regular Time Capacity in Hour per Employee	3	3	3	3
Part Time - Regular Time Cost per Hour	12	12	12	12
Part Time - Undertime Cost per Hour	5	5	5	5
Part Time - Overtime Capacity in Hour per Employee	3	3	3	3
Part Time - Overtime Cost per Hour	18	18	18	18
Part Time - Hiring Cost per Employee	20	20	20	20
Part Time - Dismissal Cost per Employee	50	50	50	50
Part Time - Maximum Number of Employee Allowed	5	5	5	5
Part Time - Minimum Number of Employee Allowed	0	0	0	0
Initial Inventory (+) or Backorder (-)	10			
Maximum Ending Inventory Allowed	M	M	M	M
Minimum Ending Inventory (Safety Stock)	10	10	10	10
Unit Inventory Holding Cost	15	15	15	15
Maximum Subcontracting Allowed	M	M	M	M
Unit Subcontracting Cost	50	50	50	50
Maximum Backorder Allowed	M	M	M	M
Unit Backorder Cost	20	20	20	20
Maximum Lost-Sales Allowed	M	M	M	M
Unit Lost-Sales Cost	30	30	30	30
Other Unit Production Cost				
Capacity Requirement in Hour per Unit	1	1	1	1

Figure 18.3

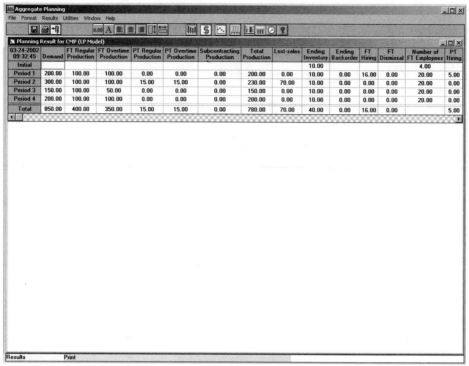

Figure 18.4

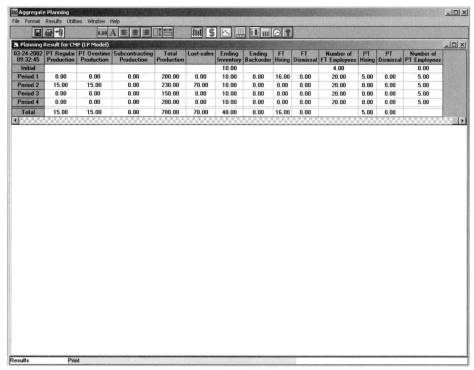

Figure 18.5

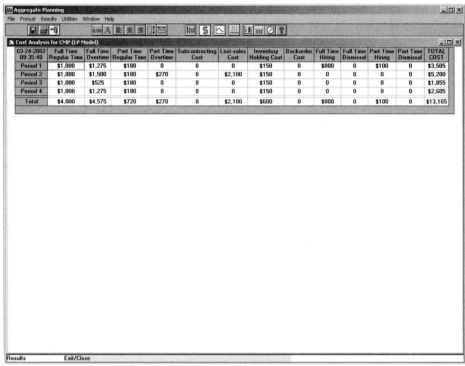

Figure 18.6

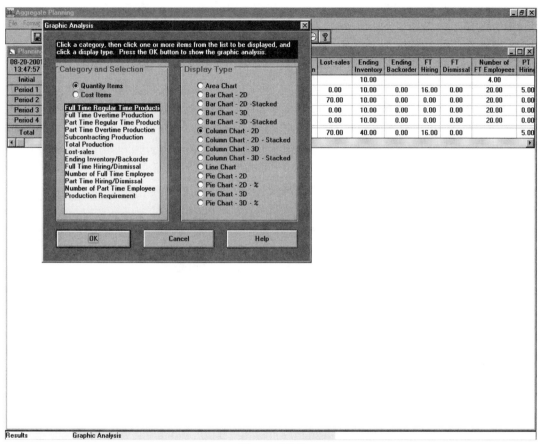

Figure 18.7

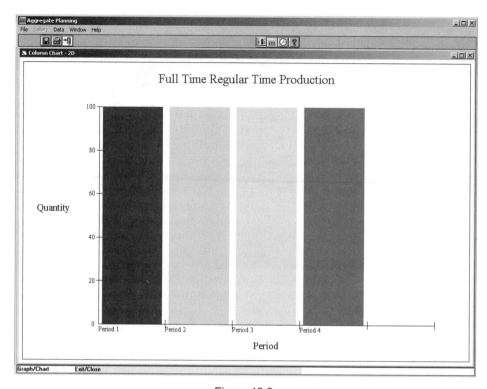

Figure 18.8

CHAPTER 19

Facility Location and Layout (FLL)

This programming module, Facility Location and Layout (FLL), solves facility location, functional layout, and line balancing problems.

The FLL program has the following capabilities:

Facility Location problems:
- Solve single and multiple locations
- Use three different distance measures

Functional Layout problems:
- Use 2-way, 3-way, and a combination of these two departmental exchanges to solve for a better layout
- Use three different distance measures

Line Balancing problems:
- Use 10 heuristics, best bud search, or COMSOAL type generation to solve line balancing

LINE BALANCING

The line balancing technique assigns tasks to workstations in an assembly line design based on precedence relationships among the tasks. Here the design of the line is to have the minimum number of workstations for a given cycle time or production requirement.

CMP is designing a new assembly line for their newest nightstand. There are nine tasks to perform. Figure 19.1 shows the tasks and their precedent relationship along with the task time.

Task Number	Task Name	Task Time in minute	Task Isolated (Y/N)	Immediate Successor (task number separated by ,)
1	Task 1	2	No	2
2	Task 2	4	No	3,4,5
3	Task 3	6	No	7
4	Task 4	4	No	6
5	Task 5	7	No	6
6	Task 6	3	No	8
7	Task 7	5	No	8
8	Task 8	4	No	9
9	Task 9	3	No	

Figure 19.1

To solve this problem, open WinQSB and select **Facility Location and Layout** module. Click on **File** and select **New Problem** from the toolbar. In the problem specification menu, select Line Balancing as the **Problem Type**. The **Number of Operational Tasks** is 9, and the **Time Unit** is a minute. Once this information has been entered, click **OK** (Figure 19.2). The screen will display data input in spreadsheet form. Enter the data as shown in Figure 19.3. On the toolbar, click on **Solve and Analyze,** and select **Solve the Problem**. The next screen will display the menu for line balancing solution options. In this example, for the **Solution Method**, the heuristic procedure is selected; **Primary Heuristic** is Longest Task Time. For the **Tie Breaker**, random option is selected. The **Cycle Time** is 12 minutes (Figure 19.4). Now click **OK** to get the solution. Figure 19.5 displays the solution for this line-balancing problem. Now click on **Results** on the toolbar, and select **Show Line Balancing Summary**. Figure 19.6 gives the summary of the line balancing design. Click on **Results** on the tool bar, and select **Show Line Layout in Graph** and you will see the graphical design of the line balancing (Figure 19.7).

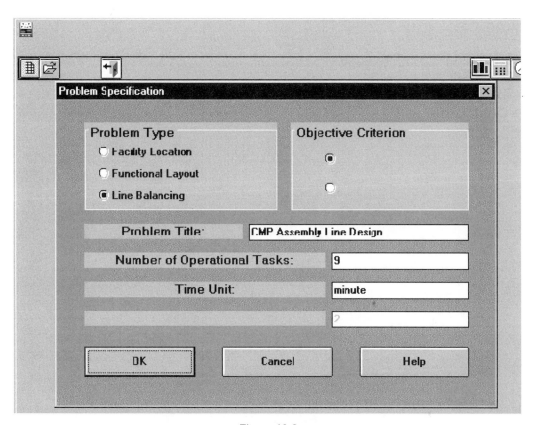

Figure 19.2

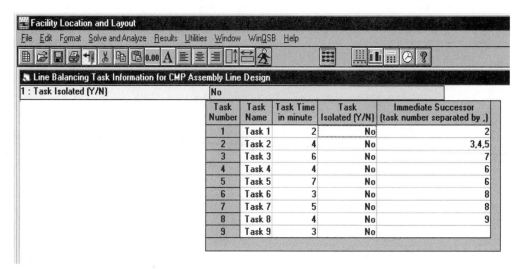

Figure 19.3

Figure 19.4

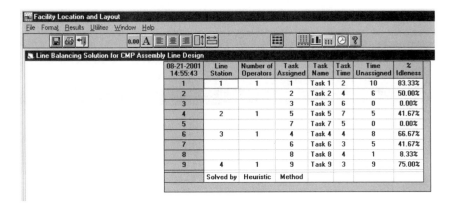

Figure 19.5

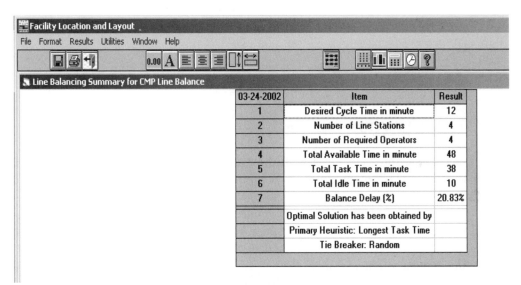

Figure 19.6

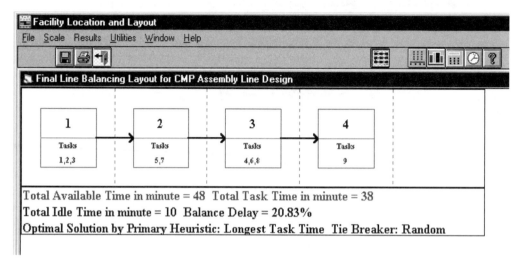

Figure 19.7

FUNCTIONAL LAYOUT

A functional layout problem deals with the arrangement of functional departments in relative locations. This module uses a Computerized Relative Allocation of Facilities Technique (CRAFT) type algorithm.

CMP wants to explore a layout for one of their shops with six departments. Information regarding the departments, their size, current locations, and the flow of material from each department to other departments are shown in Figure 19.8. To explore this layout problem, open WinQSB, select **Facility Location and Layout** module. Now click on **File** and select **New Problem** on the toolbar, and in problem specification, enter the data as shown in Figure 19.9, and click **OK**. Figure 19.10 shows the spreadsheet input form for this problem. Enter the data as shown. The next step is to solve this problem. Click on **Solve and Analyze** on the toolbar. Figure 19.11 shows the solution menu. Here in **Solution Option** select **Improve by Exchanging 2 Departments** along with selecting Rectilinear Distance as the **Distance Measure**. Click **OK** to get the solution. Figure 19.13 shows the final layout for the CMP problem. One can view the initial layout by clicking **Results** and selecting **Show Initial Layout**. Figure 19.12 shows the initial layout. To see the layout analysis, click on **Results** and select **Show Layout Analysis**. The layout analysis is shown in Figure 19.14. To see the layout distance, click on **Results** and select **Show Layout Distance**. Figure 19.15 displays the layout distance for the CMP problem.

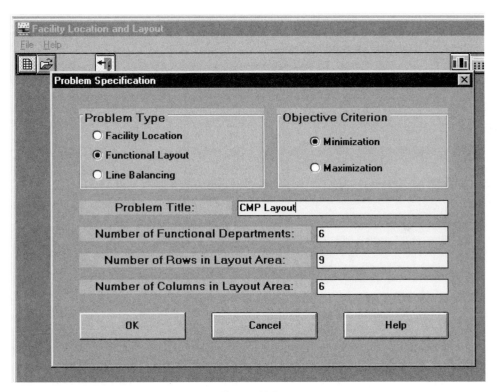

Department Number	Department Name	Location Fixed	To Dep. 1 Flow/Unit Cost	To Dep. 2 Flow/Unit Cost	To Dep. 3 Flow/Unit Cost	To Dep. 4 Flow/Unit Cost	To Dep. 5 Flow/Unit Cost	To Dep. 6 Flow/Unit Cost	Initial Layout in Cell Locations [e.g., (3,5), (1,1)-(2,4)]
1	A	no		5	78	33	78	2	(8,4)-(9,6)
2	B	no	23		34	65	33	34	(6,1)-(7,3)
3	C	no	11	35		51	23	78	(6,4)-(7,6)
4	D	Fixed	11	34	34		45	34	(3,1)-(4,3)
5	E	no	23	22	55	45		45	(3,4)-(4,6)
6	F	no	16	7	76	33	67		(1,1)-(2,3)

Figure 19.8

Figure 19.9

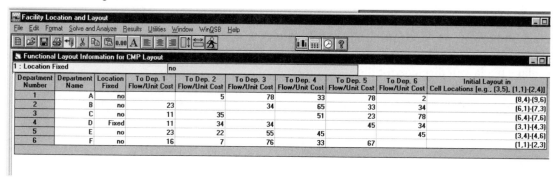

Department Number	Department Name	Location Fixed	To Dep. 1 Flow/Unit Cost	To Dep. 2 Flow/Unit Cost	To Dep. 3 Flow/Unit Cost	To Dep. 4 Flow/Unit Cost	To Dep. 5 Flow/Unit Cost	To Dep. 6 Flow/Unit Cost	Initial Layout in Cell Locations [e.g., [3,5], [1,1]-[2,4]]
1	A	no		5	78	33	78	2	[8,4]-[9,6]
2	B	no	23		34	65	33	34	[6,1]-[7,3]
3	C	no	11	35		51	23	78	[6,4]-[7,6]
4	D	Fixed	11	34	34		45	34	[3,1]-[4,3]
5	E	no	23	22	55	45		45	[3,4]-[4,6]
6	F	no	16	7	76	33	67		[1,1]-[2,3]

Figure 19.10

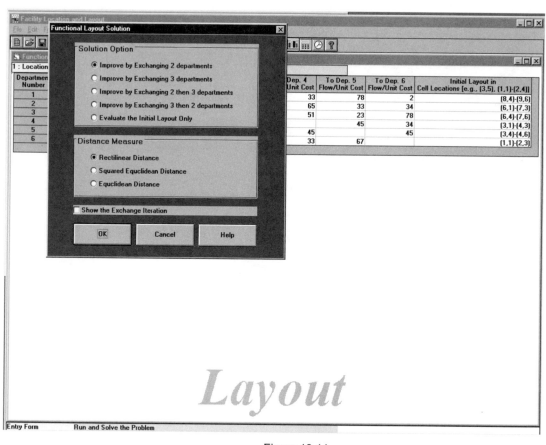

Figure 19.11

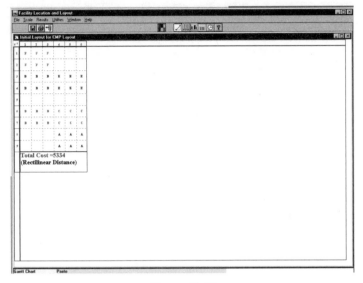

Figure 19.12

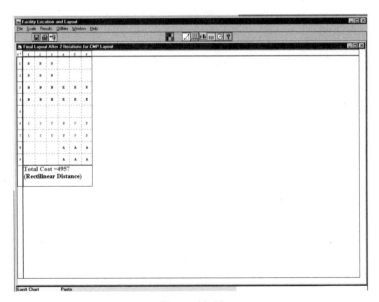

Figure 19.13

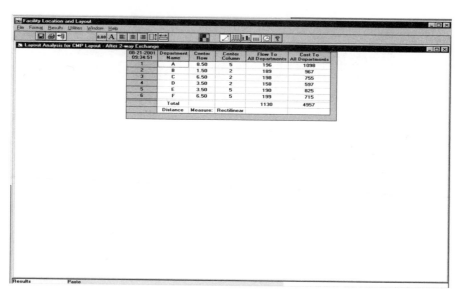

Figure 19.14

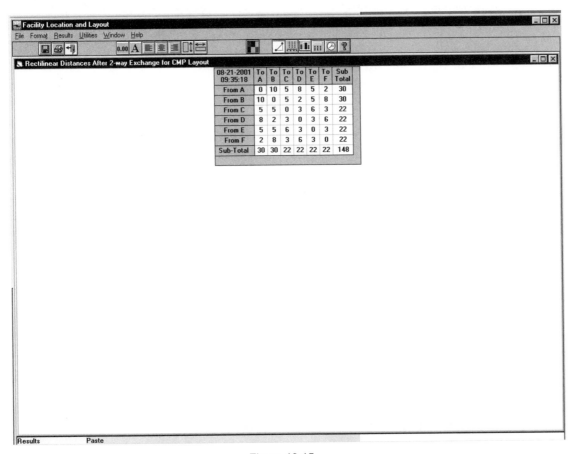

Figure 19.15

FACILITY LOCATION

A facility location problem usually considers locating new facilities with some existing facility locations. A facility could be a plant, warehouse, or distribution center, etc.

CMP wants to add two more warehouses to their current three warehouses and one plant. Information regarding the current flow of goods and location coordinates and the new location's flow of goods are shown in Figure 19.16.

To find the location for two new facilities, start WinQSB, select **Facility Location and Layout** module, click on **File,** and select **New Problem**. Click on Facility Location for **Problem Type**, and minimization for **Objective Criterion**. The **Number of Existing**

Facilities is four, and the **Number of New Facilities Planned** is two. CMP has supplied two coordinates on the map for existing facilities (Figure 19.17). Now click **OK** for the data entry, and enter the data as shown in Figure 19.18. The next step is to find the solution. Click on **Solve and Analyze,** and then click on **Solve the Problem**. The next input menu is for solution options (Figure 19.19). Click on Solve the Optimal New Location(s) for the **Solution Option** and Rectilinear Distance for the **Distance Measure**. Click **OK** for the solution. Figure 19.20 shows the solution. To see the location analysis, click **Results** from the toolbar and select **Show Location Analysis**. The resultant output is in Figure 19.21. For a graphic solution, click **Results** from the toolbar and select **Show Location in Graph**; Figure 19.22 shows the graphical location of the old four facilities and two new facilities. The next figure, Figure 19.23, shows the locations and their distances, which were obtained by clicking **Results** on the toolbar and then selecting **Show Location in Distance**.

Facility Number	Facility Name	To Existing 1 Flow/Unit Cost	To Existing 2 Flow/Unit Cost	To Existing 3 Flow/Unit Cost	To Existing 4 Flow/Unit Cost	To New 1 Flow/Unit Cost	To New 2 Flow/Unit Cost	Location X Axis	Location Y Axis
Existing 1	Existing 1		10		15	5	12	1	1
Existing 2	Existing 2	4		8		10		10	8
Existing 3	Existing 3	5	8		4		6	5	7
Existing 4	Existing 4	3	2	6		4	3	8	2
New 1	New 1	3		7			5		
New 2	New 2	4			6				

Figure 19.16

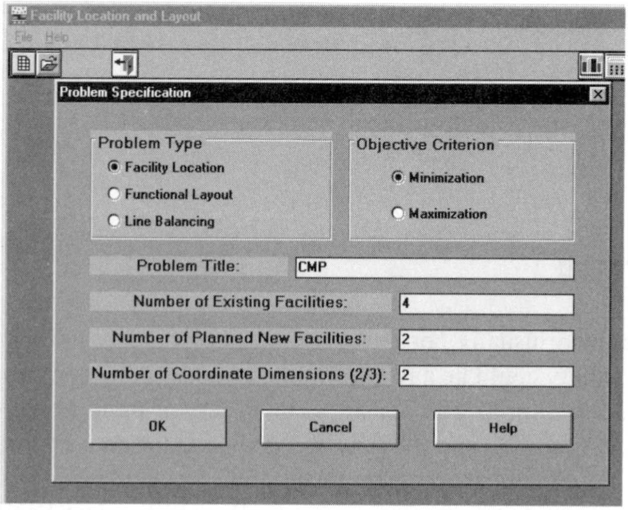

Figure 19.17

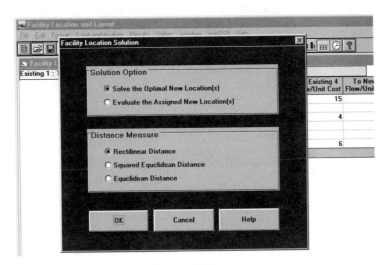

Facility Number	Facility Name	To Existing 1 Flow/Unit Cost	To Existing 2 Flow/Unit Cost	To Existing 3 Flow/Unit Cost	To Existing 4 Flow/Unit Cost	To New 1 Flow/Unit Cost	To New 2 Flow/Unit Cost	Location X Axis	Location Y Axis
Existing 1	Existing 1		10			15	5	12	1	1
Existing 2	Existing 2	4		8			10		10	8
Existing 3	Existing 3	5	8			4		6	5	7
Existing 4	Existing 4	3	2		6		4	3	8	2
New 1	New 1	3			7			5		
New 2	New 2	4				6				

Figure 19.18

Figure 19.19

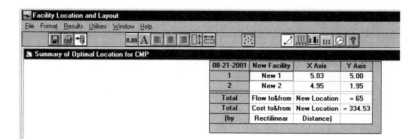

Figure 19.20

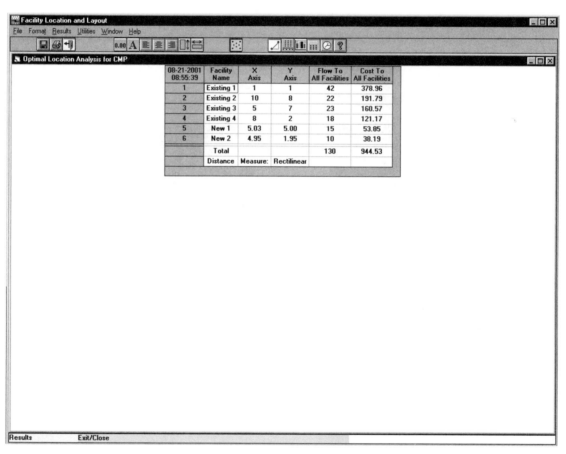

Figure 19.21

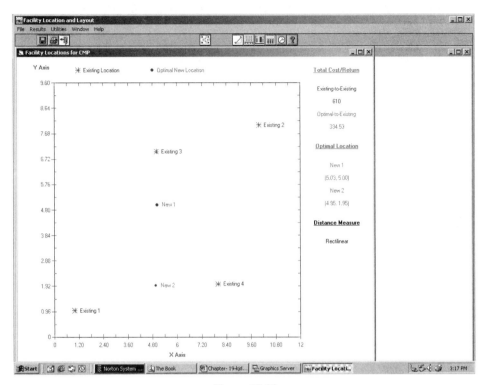

Figure 19.22

Figure 19.23

CHAPTER **20**

Material Requirements Planning (MRP)

This programming module, Material requirement planning (MRP), is a technique to determine the number of parts, components, and material needed to produce each end item. MRP also provides the schedule specifying when each of these materials, parts, and components should be produced or ordered.

This MRP module has the following capabilities:

- Perform full MRP function with input including item master, bill of material (BOM), inventory records, and master production schedule (MPS)
- Explode the MPS requirements to obtain net requirements, planned orders and projected inventory for parts and materials
- Show indented, single-level, and where-used BOM
- Show graphic product structure
- Show MRP report in part item, ABC class, source type, or material type
- Show capacity analysis
- Show cost analysis

CMP is developing a production plan for the next four months for one of its products. The product tree structure is shown in Figure 20.1. Data for this problem is in Figure 20.2. To generate the production planning for this problem, open WinQSB, and select the **Material Requirements Planning** module from the menu. Next click **File** and select **New Problem** and you will see the problem specification screen (Figure 20.3). Enter the part data (item master) as shown in Figure 20.4. The next step is to enter the product structure information. Click on **View** on the toolbar, and select the **BOM (Bill of Material)** option. Enter the data as shown in Figure 20.5. Now enter the demand for each item by clicking on **View** on the toolbar and selecting **MPS (Master Production Schedule)**. Completed input is shown in Figure 20.6. Inventory, both on hand and planned receipt information is entered by selecting **View** from the toolbar and by clicking on the **Inventory** option. Figure 20.7 shows the completed inventory data sheet. Available capacity for production for each component at CMP is entered by clicking on **View** on the toolbar and selecting the **Capacity** option. The completed data sheet is shown in Figure 20.8. By clicking **Results** on the toolbar and clicking on Show BOM (Bill of Material), one can see the product structure as shown in Figure 20.9.

Now let us solve this production planning problem for CMP. On the toolbar, click **Solve**, and select **Explode Material Requirement** to obtain the solution and analysis. In the menu displayed, select Item ID as the **Report Selection** and select @ [All Items]. Then click **OK** to get the time-phased analysis for all items (Figure 20.10).

The next screen will display the MRP report for all items with time phased gross and net requirements, inventory status, and orders released over the next four months (Figure 20.11 and 20.12). One can see the action (order) list by selecting **Show Action (order) List** on the **Results** on the toolbar (Figure 20.13), capacity analysis by selecting **Show Capacity Analysis** (Figure 20.14), and cost analysis by selecting **Show Cost Analysis** (Figure 20.15).

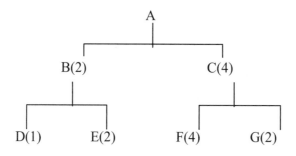

Figure 20.1

her

No	Item ID	ABC Class	Source Code	Material Type	Unit Measure	Lead Time	Lot Size	LS Multiplier	Scrap %	Annual Demand	Unit Cost	Setup Cost	Holding Annual Cost	Shortage Annual Cost	Item Description	Other Note
1	A	A	Made	FG	Each	2	LFL			5000	500	100	25	M		
2	B	A	Made	Assembly	Each	1	LFL				100	60	25	M		
3	C	B	Made	Semi	Each	1	LFL				120	50	30	M		
4	D	B	Made	Semi	Each	1	PPB		2	2000	40	5	10	M		
5	E	B	Made	Comp	Each	2	EOQ		2		45	20	11	M		
6	F	B	Made	Comp	Each	1	EOQ		1	1000	50	40	12.5	M		
7	G	C	Buy	Comp	Each	2	EOQ		1	500	10	35	2.5	M		

Figure 20.2

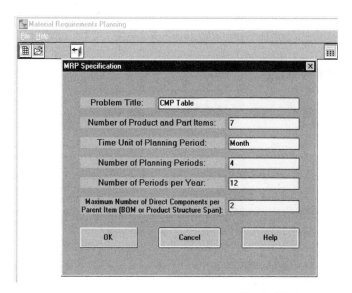

Figure 20.3

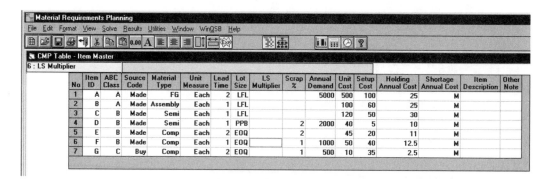

No	Item ID	ABC Class	Source Code	Material Type	Unit Measure	Lead Time	Lot Size	LS Multiplier	Scrap %	Annual Demand	Unit Cost	Setup Cost	Holding Annual Cost	Shortage Annual Cost	Item Description	Other Note
1	A	A	Made	FG	Each	2	LFL			5000	500	100	25	M		
2	B	A	Made	Assembly	Each	1	LFL				100	60	25	M		
3	C	B	Made	Semi	Each	1	LFL				120	50	30	M		
4	D	B	Made	Semi	Each	1	PPB		2	2000	40	5	10	M		
5	E	B	Made	Comp	Each	2	EOQ		2		45	20	11	M		
6	F	B	Made	Comp	Each	1	EOQ		1	1000	50	40	12.5	M		
7	G	C	Buy	Comp	Each	2	EOQ		1	500	10	35	2.5	M		

Figure 20.4

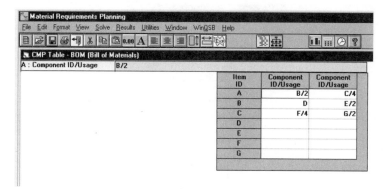

Item ID	Component ID/Usage	Component ID/Usage
A	B/2	C/4
B	D	E/2
C	F/4	G/2
D		
E		
F		
G		

Figure 20.5

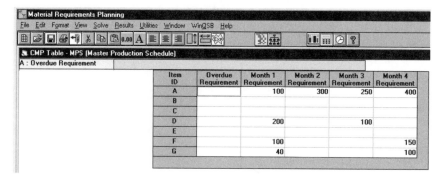

Item ID	Overdue Requirement	Month 1 Requirement	Month 2 Requirement	Month 3 Requirement	Month 4 Requirement
A		100	300	250	400
B					
C					
D		200		100	
E					
F		100			150
G		40			100

Figure 20.6

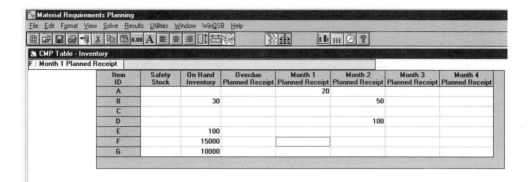

Figure 20.7

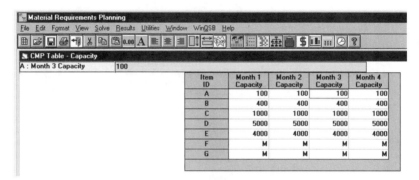

Figure 20.8

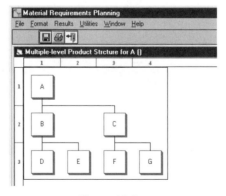

Figure 20.9

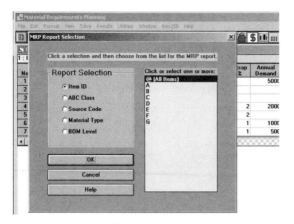

Figure 20.10

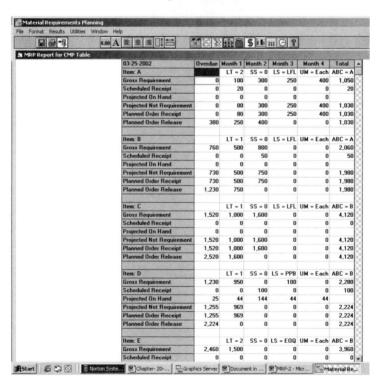

Figure 20.11

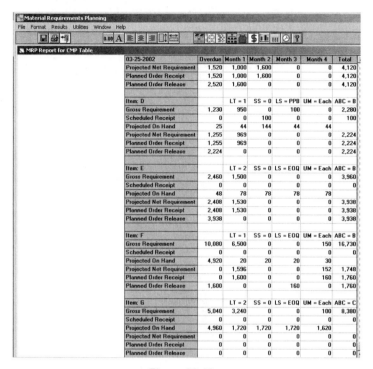

Figure 20.12

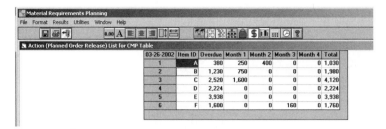

Figure 20.13

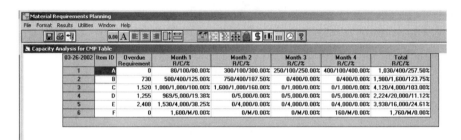

Figure 20.14

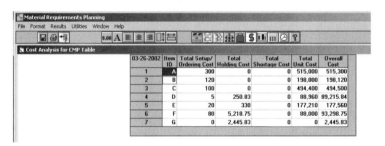

Figure 20.15